*Under
the
Cabin Lamp*

UNDER
the
CABIN LAMP

A Yachtsman's Gossip,
with pen drawings and oil sketches
by the author

H. ALKER TRIPP

Lodestar Books

First published 1950 by Iliffe and Sons Ltd
for Yachting World magazine
This edition published 2014 by
Lodestar Books
71 Boveney Road, London, SE23 3NL, United Kingdom

www.lodestarbooks.com

A CIP catalogue record for this book
is available from the British Library

ISBN 978-1-907206-20-7

Typeset by Lodestar Books in Equity

Printed in Spain by Graphy Cems, Navarra

All papers used by Lodestar Books
are sourced responsibly

Contents

Part I—Thames Mouth

Part II—Down Channel

Part III — Those Happier Days

Preface

"Nothing of high mark in this," said Charles Dickens, in one of his books; and his words certainly apply in the present case. The ordinary yachtsman has many yarns to tell, but all that gossip is of a very homely kind. He has cruised from port to port; he very likely has sailed in big yachts as well as little. He has certainly been disreputable while cruising, with horny hands and probably two or three days' stubble on his chin; and he may also have been neat and respectable on shining decks at Cowes. He has 'taken it green' when he has thrashed to windward down-Channel; and he has idled on halcyon seas and landlocked waters. Under sail he has dodged the big shipping and the tugs and lighters in busy ports; and he has ghosted in moonlight on deserted seaways.

Recollections of this kind are told under the cabin lamp, when the sails are furled and the anchor down. We all have our own stories and topics, and here are a few of mine. I am bound to admit, with many apologies, that there is 'nothing of high mark' in any of these pages; but, I hope that they carry with them something of the smell of salt water and the wind.

ALKER TRIPP
Thames Ditton, Surrey, 1950.

PART I

Thames Mouth

Up Thames Mouth

THE WIND HAD FAVOURED US AT FIRST. From Ramsgate a strongish breeze from the south-south-west had sent the yacht along to the North Foreland in smooth water, under the lee of those low chalk cliffs. Off the Foreland itself there was quite a heavy, but short-lived, popple of crested seas, one or two of which broke right on board. Skies were dull, and the seascape a sort of dirty grey.

In Margate Roads the seas became smoother again, and, with the mainsheet eased well away, we reeled the knots off in fine style. The tidal stream was still contrary, but the yacht lay over from that stiff breeze and cut the green water as with a knife. She was splendid. Margate Pier was soon left astern, and the little harbour—dry now at low tide. This good breeze would carry us into the Thames before nightfall, and we would anchor off the Blyth Sands.

"There's no sense in standing offshore into the rougher water of Prince's Channel," I had suggested when we were off the Foreland, and my shipmate had agreed. For that reason we were now laying our course for the Gore Channel. We could just make out the outline of the Margate Hook Beacon which, though it looks so large and massive when one lands at low water, is a very paltry object at first espied on the long sea line. Away to northward we could see the shipping of the main channel, or sometimes only the smudges of smoke when the vessels themselves were invisible, hull-down. A typical Thames-mouth day this, with its grey sky and green-grey sea, and the wind blowing seaward.

This fairway is beset by shoals. Through the Gore and Horse Channels the way was well buoyed, but beyond them was a great stretch of unbuoyed shoal water, where awkward little patches like the Pudding Pan and the Spaniard dry out at low-water springs, and lie in wait just nicely awash between half-tide and low water. Even a yacht of our light draught would bump them.

Under low cloud the sea looked dark and desolate. We ticked off the buoys one after another as we passed them, and the beacon was soon abeam. Coming out of the cold wind, when one went below to plot the course, the cabin seemed surprisingly warm. The noise of the water sweeping by was a gurgle, loud and continual down there, with an occasional *splosh* as the yacht, shouldering over some larger wave than usual, came down with a bump on the other side of it. The angle of the table to the cabin registered a healthy heel from this vigorous breeze.

Our course was perhaps unorthodox, carrying us as it did right across the shoals, but the tide was now making. We felt safe enough, despite the fact that, since the flood had begun to sweep Thames-ward, the seas had started to foam up and break in caps of surf. We wanted, if possible, to be at anchor before dark, because it is so much easier to select a snug spot by daylight, and a snug berth is so important when there is steamer traffic about.

"We'd better keep the lead going," I said, "and keep knowing, as far as possible, just where we are. We don't want to bump, and we're quite all right if we keep in the best of it." So the lead went flopping time after time into the water, and time after time the dripping line came in through one's fingers. It is a game that can become wearisome when long protracted. Some of the Whitstable 'yawls' (which are cutter-rigged, despite their name) were dotted about here and there, but they were no guide to us. The oyster dredgers know their own 'grounds' as a gardener knows his own garden, and they can exploit every little swatchway of deep water.

In a couple of hours, during which we hardly touched a sheet, we had sailed outside the Columbine buoy, past Warden Point, and had brought the earth cliffs of the Isle of Sheppey abeam. We were heading away for the Jenkin Swatchway, across the well-buoyed fairway, for the River Medway.

"If one can't see the buoys, one can always see the barges," my shipmate said; "the barge traffic in and out of that river seems to be unceasing." The horizon was perioded by these sailing barges, while nearer at hand were two or three Leigh bawleys, each with topsail set and with one reef in the mainsail. An Atlantic Transport liner was away on the sealine in the direction of the Nore, and a couple of black-funnelled tramp steamers, followed by some large ocean freighter with a mass of derricks, were making Thames-ward. In the direction of Sheerness was a destroyer moving at speed.

"Back to modern civilisation," my shipmate said, as we rapidly converged with that narrow artery at the Nore which takes all the traffic of the world's greatest port. "What an extraordinary contrast. In the shoal-waters we only meet the ships and the business of a couple of hundred years ago, quiet and ancient and unhurried, and there..."

One or two barges, flying light, were beating up in company with us

As he pointed, my eye centred, not on the traffic, but on the low sky, which was obviously brightening to westward—it was clearing. We should have a fine evening. But—I hoped not, but—yes, sure enough, it was; the wind was veering. It was drawing ahead.

"Come on," I said, "we've got to close-haul her; our lazy life is over. It's going to be a turn to windward all the way up. And we've got to work for our living if we intend to get up beyond Hole Haven to-night."

The wind freshened as it veered, and began to knock up quite a bit of sea. This was of the true steep Thames-mouth type. We were soon both in oilskins, and the spray was flying. The wind was now due west.

We decided that we would push on. We would not curtail our intended passage, despite the fact that—for a snug berth—we should have to go beyond the Blyth sands and bring up in the barge anchorage in the Lower Hope. With this wind due west Sea Reach would be no place for us if we wanted to sleep in peace. The yacht would be pitching, bowsprit-under, all the time.

"We'll carry a strong tide under us," I said; "it's fairly sluicing up London-ward now; and we'll have a jolly good shot for the Lower Hope. If we fail, we can find our way to a reasonably decent berth in the Medway in the dark. And the wind may fall lighter with the ebb."

It was not dusk as yet; we had a couple of good hours' daylight in hand, and we meant to make the most of them. "Sail as if you were racing," I said to my shipmate, who, now at the helm, looked as intent and purposeful as anyone could wish. "It is concentration that does it," I reminded him, with various other such-like gibes—for he knew all these things as well as I did. "Keep your mind on your job, and you'll get your supper." The Lower Hope would be as snug as anyone could wish in this wind.

The yacht lifted skew-wise over the steep waves, and plunged with a resounding smack into the trough. The helmsman was handling her admirably, but the waves killed her speed and deadened her life. The swept spray stung; it hit us solid and trickled down us in great rivulets. The sun came out at last, low down, and shining full in our eyes, and the wind hardened still more. We talked at first, but we got tired of the effort in that fusillade of spray, and soon the only words were—at very long intervals—"What about it now? A little longer on this tack? Or shall we go about?" "Ready about, then; lee ho!"

One or two barges, flying light, were beating up in company with us. They looked very solid and powerful, and were certainly keeping the sea in its place. But our own little packet, drenched though she was in spray, was keeping pace with them—not too bad a showing under these conditions. When one looked astern now, the seascape was a picture, with the low sunlight so strong upon the tawny brown sails that looked the warmer and the brighter by contrast with the retreating clouds. And the foam-capped sea was reflecting strong facets of deep blue here and there from the clearing sky. This was a magnificent evening.

Southend pier was now astern, and the Chapman pile lighthouse could be seen on the north shore. Across and across the wide reach we thrashed, sometimes dry for awhile, and sometimes throwing the spray in sheets, till the mainsail was drenched half-way up, and the water was running in streams from the boom. I was by this time taking my own turn at the helm, and I well remember the uplift and pleasurable excitement of the passage. The yacht felt more buoyant again, for the seas were rather longer and less vicious, and she seemed, as a yacht always does under such conditions, so marvellously game, so plucky, so splendid. We had forgotten all about supper and bed in this thrilling little race with time and tide.

Against the setting sun were silhouetted the chimneys and oil reservoirs of Thames Haven, and we thrashed resolutely on. We should not reach the Lower Hope by sunset. If, however, some barges were at anchor there we could pick up a position slightly inshore of them by the lead, and could thus feel pretty secure.

The sun was down, and darkness well-nigh upon us. The tide would soon be turning; this was a neck-and-neck race.

"Never mind," I said, as yet once again I put the helm down and the yacht went about. "If this breeze holds we can still carry on over the first half-hour of ebb, before the tide really begins to run. I think we shall do it."

We seemed an everlastingly long while in closing the western shore of the Lower Hope, thrashing along close-hauled, but in definitely smoother water now. With that sense of pleasurable achievement, which is always present, however small the task, we slid at last in among the anchored barges somewhere off Coal House Battery, and, by the lead, we let go. The sunset was over, and the night had begun.

"The tide's well away now," my shipmate commented, as he hung the riding light on the forestay. "We had mighty little margin; and the wind is taking-off."

The night was quiet in this snug spot. We laid out the kedge shoreward, and furled the mainsail. It was wet with dew as well as with salt-water.

"A fine day to-morrow," we said as we went below, and a glance at the rising barometer endorsed the suggestion. In the very best of spirits we prepared our evening meal.

And the next day we were in Lower Pool, off Wapping.

Cross-Purposes

IT IS ALWAYS A PITY TO GET AT CROSS-PURPOSES. But the thing is sometimes inevitable; it simply occurs. Were it not for the rule of the road ashore and the Board of Trade rules at sea, cross-purposes would become so acute that many of us would never survive to settle their merits. And even as it is, we do not always escape from getting involved in crossing one another.

These cross-purposes at sea are of many kinds. For instance, there are the people who will use boats but do not know a first thing about their management. Such people are apt to be a particular danger if—as is only natural—the other party assumes that the conduct of the on-coming vessel will be normal. Very likely the boat is handled quite rationally until it is at close quarters; and then does something quite amazing. The margin of time for coping with the situation may by then be very narrow.

The obvious ignoramus is less of a danger. E. F. Knight wrote an amusing account of his contact with a Bank Holiday crowd on the Upper Thames when he was sailing in a brisk breeze. The river was crowded with skiffs and dinghies, all in very inexpert hands. He found that "he or she who held the yoke-lines," on seeing the sailing boat rushing through the water towards the skiff, under a great sail, got flurried, put the rudder first one way and then the other, and "gave contradictory orders to an unmanageable crew." First the crew would pull ahead in panic, and then—just as the helmsman of the sailing boat was preparing to pass under their stern—they would of a sudden cease rowing or back-water. It required all Knight's skill and judgment to avoid collision. He was turning to windward at the time, and a boat-load of Cockney youths and maidens, pulling manfully in mid-stream, thought that he was crossing and recrossing the river of set purpose to annoy them. The mystery of tacking was beyond their ken. So, in terms more forcible than polite, they shouted to him to "sail straight, instead of zigzagging in that silly drunken fashion from one side of the river to the other."

Another source of cross-purposes is misconception as to the relative status of the two converging vessels. The description sounds rather a mouthful; but we have all experienced the fact. For myself I have suffered, and I have offended also. A cruising yacht in narrow waters will always give way to a large steam vessel, and

Cross-purposes of sailing vessels and power vessels are perpetual and everlasting

she certainly ought to. But what is a large steam vessel? I remember in Sea Reach (near Southend) a little rat of a steamer standing straight at us, and expecting us to break our tack and keep clear. We didn't; we held our course. I clearly recall the panic fashion in which the skipper spun the spokes of his wheel. He had plenty of sea room, and his conduct in trying to bully us into going about for him was inexcusable.

Then there are races. Anyone with any self-respect and decency at all will keep so completely clear of a race as to be no possible hindrance or anxiety to any competitor. I have in my time put my yacht aground in order to keep clear of a race in very narrow waters; it is true that the tide was rising, and I am not, there-fore, claiming the credit or crown of a martyr. On another occasion I remember that we divagated into a blind creek in order to leave the main fairway completely clear for a race of small boats. But my shipmate and I have not always done the right thing. Very well do I remember an occasion long ago when, after passing a race of small yachts at a respectful distance we stood boldly across the bows of an isolated yacht that was on port tack. She was so very far apart from the race that she appeared to be sailing on her own. She had (as we afterwards saw) a race flag at her truck; but it was completely hidden by the gaff.

Finally, the cross-purposes of sailing vessels turning to windward and power vessels that go straight are perpetual and everlasting. By day, and with plenty of sea room, there should be little trouble. But even then cross-purposes are not unknown. Some years ago I was in a yacht bound for Plymouth, and turning to windward over a lee-going tide in the open channel. A large steamer shaped course to cross the yacht's bows at very close quarters indeed, but the yacht (rightly, and as the book of words ordains) held her course and speed. Sharply the steamer slewed round and passed under her stern.

But most of all these cross-purposes arise in narrow fairways which carry a heavy steamer traffic. The Thames is perhaps the best possible case in point. From the North Foreland to London itself the fairway is a narrow one for large vessels, and the yacht which is properly handled is always at pains not to incommode a shipmaster or pilot navigating a large vessel under such conditions. This is easy enough by day, but by night it is difficult, because one cannot compute the precise direction of the steamer's course with any real accuracy. On a cloudy night the lights alone are visible, and course and speed are both difficult to judge. The yacht which is on the wind all the way from the Tongue Lightship will very likely encounter the whole procession of steamers which has left London at high water. For her own safety she is determined to keep clear of them, rules or no rules. She is standing across the bows of distant ones and under the stern of others all the time, and she gets a bit tired of them. I have done it often enough, and I know. The first glimpse of dawn is a godsend.

Night on the London Sea Lane

BOUND SEAWARD, THE YACHT HAD LEFT LONDON with the morning tide. Day was nearly over now and, as five hours of contrary tide were still before us, we hoped that the freshening breeze would decide to hold. It might peter out at nightfall. From golden sunlight in the Lower Hope we passed to sunset soon after we had opened Sea Reach. Evening came very quickly over the spirit of everything, and the seascape was coloured with the cold grey-blue of twilight. After reaching down to the Mucking we had now squared away and were running free. Over the Blyth Sand barges and bawleys were bringing up in number for the night; sails were being furled everywhere, and riding lights set. The sight of it suggested the idea of a snug supper and a quiet turn-in, a fancy with its own allurement in this chilly nightfall. But we were outward bound. Waste of the fair wind would be really sinful, and the yacht, with a trusty breeze in her canvas now, swung resolutely on seaward. Lights began to twinkle from Leigh and Southend, and the steamships showed coloured eyes of green and red as they thrust vigorously by. The traffic to and from the Port of London was, as always, in full tide. Our own side-lights had been trimmed and lighted, and were now set in their brackets on the shrouds. Day was finished; this was full night.

The Chapman pile lighthouse was astern, and the next important light would be the Nore.

We had settled down to night conditions. The gurgle and the *splash-splash-splash* at the bow were pleasant sounds. The binnacle was alight, and the cabin-lamp also; while the yacht herself seemed to acquire a separate confident personality as she plugged forward into the gloom. I conned her lovingly as I stood at the helm—those sails of hers, dark in the night above, and that little square of the cabin-doorway (clear-cut with the light within) below them. Inside, on the cabin table, the chart was spread out; the big parallel rulers and the dividers lay upon it. The doors of the cabin were open, for the lamp itself is beneath the helmsman's line of sight, being shut off by the cabin roof, and, so long as the direct light does not shine in his eyes, the mere glimmer of warmth dazzles him no more than does the binnacle. He wants his eyesight unimpaired for, as often as not, he is look-out as well as helmsman, and he wants eyes in the back of his head as much as in front. We were not showing a white stern-light, but a lamp was kept at hand for the purpose if need be.

Course had been laid by compass for the Nore. In the jewellery of yellow lights that studded the waterway the light was not yet visible. It would only be a pin-point as yet, gleaming every half-minute. But... yes, there it was! The binnacle could be ignored now.

"Pleasanter to steer for a mark than by compass," my shipmate said. "And less exacting, too."

Meanwhile this steamer traffic of the Port of London was incessant, and it wanted watching. While we had been still skirting the edge of the Blyth Sand we had been clear of the mid-fairway; but now, with the Jenkin Swatchway abeam, we were converging with it, in the orthodox steamer-track for the Nore. Ship after ship would rise in the distance, her green and red lights a-shine; if, as she approached, one of them disappeared, she was passing us safely. If both remained, glaring more and more balefully bright as she mounted into size and shape, then, obviously, look out for her!

Just such a one came up behind us here, full and truly astern.

"Look at her," I said, " dead astern, following our very track, and close on us. She hasn't a notion we're here!"

The yacht must have been totally invisible to the look-out of the steamer, for the moment our stern-light was shown she slewed round with quite a sharp turn to northward before settling down on her new course.

The Nore was soon abeam, and the tangle of fairway lights of the Medway — red and white. The traffic streamed on unabated, but it called for nothing save a strict look-out, and was no anxiety. With our wind free, we could steer as straight a course as any power vessel; the nuisance is when the yacht is beating, and must be perpetually cutting athwart the course of everything else.

The yacht was moving with an easy swing over the waves, and the glimmer of the foam in her wake was a dull grey on the black water. The gurgle of the bow wave was a pleasant sound. Yes, this was a perfect night.

The Girdler Light Vessel (now gone) would be the next important light, distant about eleven miles, and by compass again the yacht's course was laid. In a straight line into the open seaways of the night she would carry on, perfectly confident that, in due course, the light would glitter up right over the bowsprit.

One is apt to take so much for granted. Here, in the midnight, it seemed no marvel that the yacht should be able to hold an assured course. Yet the land is lost to sight, and the seaway for the next five and twenty miles will be shoaled on all hands with sandbanks and shingles, the grave of ships. Heavy toll has been exacted here of the ships of London since London was first a port at all.

What was the hour now? I glanced down at the cabin clock; it was midnight. The Girdler had by this time been sighted some ten miles distant, and the Red

One of them, which had been a mere smudge, became a ship of fairyland

Sand light almost as soon. By half-past one that ten miles had been wiped out, and the Light Vessel was close aboard of us—its great beam, shining like a searchlight, dazzled one's eyes more and more. The darkness was that of the pit as soon as the light was obscured.

On the same course as ourselves, two steamers had been steering straight for the Light Vessel, and passing it at close quarters. Past the Light Vessel we also swung. One of the steamers, which had been a mere smudge in the darkness, noticeable only by reason of a pinpoint or two of white or coloured light, became a ship of fairyland in a moment. The searchlight was on her. Every detail of her shone and glistened against a black background of night, as she chug-chugged away down the broad fairway. The breeze blew, the light dropped farther and farther astern, and night was again as black as ever.

But the tide which had been helping us through the night was now about to turn against us. Before we made good the distance to the whistle buoy at the South Shingles, the hostile tide was running strongly. When we hauled the East Tongue abeam, the time was half-past three. Course was changed for the N.E. Spit; and, in a broken seaway, a seaway of wind-creased water, we drove through the darkness.

"Dawn, surely."

Gripping the coaming to steady ourselves as the vessel rolled, we scanned the sky northeastward. On a clear night the first glimpse of dawn is always that dim tinge of paler blue low along the sea-line, faint almost beyond recognition; and one likes to be the first to spot it. Yes, it was there.

Limping Home

WE SAIL FORTH IN PERFECT TRIM, but sometimes we return in no high feather. To come limping home is a wretched business. True, it is not by any means the worst home-coming that a yacht can contrive. Worst of all home-comings is that of the poor vessel that cannot even limp—some yacht that had set sail proudly with canvas white in the sunshine, and comes home in tow—dismasted perhaps, or so water-logged that she will not handle.

Pathetic also is the little ship that, although badly winged, makes port somehow and somewhere, unaided; but at the same time she wears an air of gallantry also.

Obviously, there is nothing heroic about a man who goes to sea with rotten gear, and then plumes himself on the address and skill with which he surmounted difficulties which were really of his own silly creation. If a man plays that little game he will do it once too often. In sheltered waters there is no real hurt to be taken; but out on the sea no degree of sureness can be too sure.

How, then, is the mariner to make really sure? He can only carry his sureness to a certain pitch, and then leave the rest to luck. The sweet little cherub that sits up aloft is a chancy creature. The cherub sometimes looks after Jack when Jack has been as improvident as the very devil; and sometimes the cherub turns nasty when Jack has really deserved the best.

Always, when misfortune *does* overtake us, we can be sure of finding charitable friends ready to put the whole blame on us and to let the cherub off scot-free. Take a small instance. Once when our dinghy parted towage, a self-righteous person at a later date told me that he had "never known a new rope break." Maybe. Not being a millionaire, I cannot say. We cannot have brand-new painters every time we set sail. And that is just where the difficulty occurs. Deterioration is gradual; and how can one tell with sufficient accuracy when the precise moment for condemnation has arrived? It so happened that both painters were found on examination afterwards to have been in good condition, and I dare say that—even if brand-new—they would have parted just the same.

It is a coincidence, too, that on that particular occasion (which was at the end of the season) some of the halliards were finished, and were to be renewed at the next fitting out. These had remained intact while two of the staunchest pieces of rope that the little yacht boasted were snapped like pack-thread. It only shows what a lottery these things are.

The proper method of judging a rope is to twist it against the lay, thus opening to view the inner side of the strands. If they are frayed and dry-looking, renewal is due. Experience teaches judgment; but there is no final guarantee—never.

Take another example. In just the same way I, like many others, have had a mainsail 'blowed away.' It happened like this. My shipmate and I had anchored off Brightlingsea for the night, intending to sail to Harwich in the morning. Turning out of our bunks at 5 o'clock in the morning, we could see that we had a dirty day: wind was due north, and squally. With two reefs in the mainsail, the yacht raced off through the broken shoalwater; but the sea was something else. Close-hauled we were beating, and the spray cut like a knife. After some hours, we knew we should not reach Harwich: the waves were breaking on the yacht with a thump, and each time she was stopped. This wind seemed most of a gale, and our nearest haven would be Brightlingsea or Mersea. So, with the wind over our stern, we flew— whence we had come.

We were over-canvassed. Back to the Bench Head buoy, we shortened the sheet to bring her on the wind. At that same moment, there was a savage flapping of loose sail: our mainsail was torn and slit, from leech to luff! We were being driven to the lee shore, and we had no trysail. But we sprang to bend our biggest jib, to make a mainsail of sorts, as best we could. With this jury-rig, the yacht was under *some* control. But we could not weather Sales Point, or reach our haven: we must run now for the Crouch.

To be wrecked on the Foulness Sand was our fear: we could see the long white line where waves were breaking. An anxious time it was, but we crept toward the

Somewhere and somehow she comes limping home!

mouth of the Crouch. There the tide was too strong for us, and we decided to 'cast anchor.' But the anchor was not holding. We hauled away at the cable, and as the shackle clanked on the fairlead, we could see that the flukes of the anchor had gone! How it happened we do not know to this day. No mainsail, and now no anchor! The kedge would not hold; so we tried to sail again. By luck we were able to keep clear of the lee shore, and the tide would soon be turning. In fact we managed to creep to Burnham after nightfall, and picked up a mooring.

The morning was bright and quiet. When I unbent that mainsail and carried it up to a sailmaker's loft, one of my first questions was in regard to its condition. "Do you consider," I asked, "that this accident was due to the condition of the sail?" The old fellow fingered the canvas all over carefully, and looked at it through his spectacles. "I certainly wouldn't say that" he answered. "The sail is in *good* condition. I'll machine in new cloths and the sail will be as good as ever."

It is thus not possible to be proof against the slings and arrows of outrageous fortune, however great one's foresight. All that is possible is to reduce the degree of risk to a certain irreducible minimum. We had crept limping to Burnham, but we returned home taut and sound—also with a new anchor!

All said and done, there remains that prodigious element of luck—more particularly as regards the degree of penalty exacted. Dismasting, or loss of mainsail, may mean total loss of ship and life. If the yacht is suddenly disabled when offshore rocks are directly under her lee, it may mean the end of all things, life as well as vessel. The same thing holds good of an off-shore shoal when a full gale of wind is blowing. If, on the other hand, the yacht is driven fairly on to the land, the chances are that—although the yacht will be lost—the crew may escape. If, however, she has sea-room, something in the way of jury-rig will certainly be contrived, and the ship and crew will probably be saved. The last of these yachts is the one that will come limping home; the other yachts—won't.

Another nasty uncomfortable experience is that of sailing a yacht which has sprung a serious leak. This experience is likeliest when, for reasons of economy, the owner has put to sea in a very old yacht in uncertain condition. Young men used to do this very freely, and probably still do. The leak is pretty sure to occur when the little yacht is being sorely tested by the weather. Will the leak get worse? That is the question. By bailing or pumping you can just keep pace with the inflow; but, if the hull opens up still more, you will not. Standing at the helm while your mate is feverishly bailing you feel a sudden affection for various odds and ends in the cabin which will probably be at the bottom of the sea when you and your mate are trying to get ashore in the dinghy. Yet, in the upshot, the little vessel does not go to the bottom; somewhere and somehow she comes limping home!

Nothing Doing

'NOTHING DOING' IS SOMETHING THAT DEPENDS upon whether one wants to be idle or not. Idleness may be a paradise or—the opposite. Probably there is no place where idleness can be tasted with such fullness as on the deck of an anchored yacht. The sense of luxury can creep right up to the point of perfection, in some sheltered roadstead, after a successful passage in bad weather.

On the other hand, idleness, complete and entire, can be vile. How well we all know (or used to know in pre-motor days) that sensation of being left becalmed in a swell. The wind decamps suddenly and leaves the yacht to roll and wallow, while the boom, banging from side to side, becomes a torture.

But a yacht becalmed is merely awaiting a pleasant release which will arrive at any moment: a welcome breeze will set her on her way. A yacht hove-to in a really full gale or riding to a sea-anchor is quite a different matter. Many deep-water yachtsmen have recorded their impressions—the wind has reached the full screaming sound of diabolical fury, the air is full of spray that cuts like a knife, and every monstrous white-crested wave looks as if it must surely engulf everything. Below, discomfort intolerable. Everything wet, and everything moving violently. To sit becomes impossible without being wedged firmly in, and sleep is out of the question. Mulhauser recorded the impression in *Amaryllis*, of a companion of his (who had had no previous yachting experience) during one of these extreme periods. His companion "felt convinced that nothing put together by the hands of man could possibly resist the buffeting. At the back of his mind lay the conviction that sooner or later the mast would go, ropes part, sails blow away, or the hull come to pieces." Complete enforced idleness on those terms, listening all the time for some sound (as of gear carrying away) that may spell prompt disaster—well, words simply fail.

The other end of the scale is a pleasanter subject. Voluntary idleness is almost always a luxury, especially to a real worker. There is something seductive about a yacht at anchor which enables a man, vigorous in ordinary, to relax and do nothing. "I like nothing to do and plenty of time to do it in"—that is the fitting motto. Having returned to one's floating home after a short absence, how acceptable it is! Merely to potter round the yacht, leisurely getting ready for the eventual cruise—why, it can be paradise. In theory, one is looking over one's gear and generally straightening things out, but the pauses necessary to watch the general happenings of the anchorage are long. And the sunlight and the blue water make just the setting for the lotus-eating life.

Even on a passage, moreover, the periods of enforced idleness are not always blots on the picture. In a rough seaway, as already said, they can be an abomination. But when the water is smooth and everything benign, when time does not press, and there is no indraught of tide towards an undesired coast, such periods can be a perfect delight. I can fancy myself at this moment sitting on deck two or three miles offshore and looking at Lowestoft far away and at the becalmed ketches close at hand. I looked at that view, I remember, for one whole morning without being in the least irked by it. The water was flat calm, and the sunlight unclouded. Similarly I have pleasant recollections of quietly sliding with the tide past a distant panorama of the bold clifflands of Devon, while the yacht lay basking in sunshine. It is odd how some recollections photograph themselves like that on the mind, and remain in memory so much more clearly than others; there is no particular reason, but the one day may be well remembered, the other well nigh forgotten.

I also remember a flat calm when sailing coastwise up-Channel in a 25 ton yawl. We had stood in very close to the Wight in a small off-shore breeze, and the wind had suddenly given out like the flame of a candle. The indraught in the whole bay between the Needles and St. Catherine's is strong, and in we went. I was not responsible or I should have been wondering whether to use the kedge. As it was, I stretched myself out on deck in a perfect luxury of idleness, and I have never enjoyed a morning more. The chalk cliffs in sunlight were a picture. The sea was like a mill pond, and we basked in the hot sunshine. The breeze came along later and sent us on our way rejoicing after we had basked there long enough. So why fuss?

If idle I must, give me a flat calm to idle in. Every time.

Running Amok

CRUISING YACHTS DO SOMETIMES RUN AMOK. Or shall we say rather that they *did*? With the advent of the auxiliary motor the novice has been robbed of most of the terrors of getting under way or bringing up in a crowded anchorage. Under sail, it was a very different matter. A yacht that takes charge, and really means to get into mischief, can do quite a lot of things in a little time. When she once starts running amok she can do it handsomely.

I once saw a novice bite off as pretty a little piece of trouble as anyone could hope to crowd into five brief minutes or so. He tossed his mooring buoy overboard, quite forgetting that a lee-going tide is a serious item. Without getting sufficient way on his yacht to make her handle properly, he tried to stand across the bows of an anchored smack. The smack's bowsprit was housed, or it would certainly have gored his mainsail; as it was his yacht's quarter hit the bluff bows of the smack with a sounding *conk*. The yacht, of course, swung round parallel with the smack, and the dinghy's painter snapped like pack-thread (the dinghy being round on the other side of the smack, and the tide a hot one).

The novice succeeded in getting his yacht on the wind again, but immediately found himself charging full tilt at another smack, and he had real way on his little packet this time. He tried to luff, but too late. His bowsprit snapped clean off and stood up perpendicular in the air. The yacht fell away, and the bowsprit of another smack, neatly threading itself through the topping lift of the unfortunate yacht, brought her up ignominiously, and the worse for wear.

I also have run amok in my time. In a strong easterly wind we had anchored off Heybridge Basin, on the Blackwater, and my shipmate had gone ashore for provisions. My own job was to drop the yacht a little farther down to deeper water. To get her under way would be the simplest thing in the world, because the wind was across the tide.

I got all sail on her, and the anchor was soon 'up and down,' just on the bottom. The yacht filled away and broke it out. All well, so far. I could fist up the cable in a matter of a few seconds, and run aft to the helm. Ye gods, I couldn't! The cable had jammed immovably in the anchor davit, and nothing but a hammer used lustily from underneath would release it. And the yacht was away.

His yacht's quarter hit the bluff bows of the smack with a sounding "conk"

She had turned on her heel, and had already begun to run before the wind; she was heading straight for some anchored yachts, and for a stone wall beyond—and the wind was stiff. I raced aft to the helm (not unduly perturbed as yet) to luff her up into the wind. Horror of horrors! She took no notice of the helm, and—as for luffing, "not in this life," said she.

She was running amok, good and hearty. I still tried to steer her, and by luck perhaps more than skill I avoided one yacht, and found myself going straight for another yacht and the wall—my own yacht streaking through the water now at quite a speed. I resigned myself to my fate; it would be a fearful smash. I had a vivid vision of the whole scene in my mind before it happened—and then...

Then, glory to the little gods that look after us, the anchor felt the shallower water and gradually began to bring her up; dragging through the mud more and more slowly, until the yacht grudgingly rounded up to it, her stern, as it swung, actually coming against the stone wall, but quite innocuously.

I sat down on the cabin-top for a moment, breathing as if I had been running. The relief was incredible. Next moment I had sail off her, and was away with the kedge in the dinghy. After that, it was only a matter of moments to release the anchor cable with a hammer, and to get properly under way.

The reason for the jam (a most unusual occurrence) was that the davit was old, and had been bent slightly outwards by imperceptible degrees. Then suddenly, on this occasion, it had opened still more, and the chain had dropped over the side of the sheave, and wedged itself fast. My rake's progress cannot have lasted much longer than a minute; but that minute while I was running amok was one of the longest minutes of my life.

Wintry Passage in a Bawley

A S A GUEST, I VERY HAPPILY SCRAMBLED on board of a bawley, in the Blackwater. The bawley had been a Leigh smack in her time, and had since been converted by a very old friend of mine to a yacht. The bawley is a cutter-rigged vessel, her distinguishing feature being that her mainsail has no boom.

From the shore I had spied the bawley at once, and the owner of the bawley soon espied me. I saw him clamber into his dinghy and cast off. In the shelter of a small creek, he beached his little boat, and met me with a benign and smiling countenance.

"There," said he. "And when we go back you can do the pulling. It'll take you all your time to get us there." That slow smile of his showed that he had already had a sample of it.

The bawley was rocking and rolling when we stood on board later on, for the wind was in full blast, and the sea was leaden-coloured.

"If it's going on like this, we'd better stay where we are," said the owner. "We're on a good mooring; it would take a lot to shift this mooring we're on."

I pictured the foul discomfort of an anchorage farther down, and agreed. But Nature here intervened. As we stood looking out to windward, there was a darkening of the clouds and a sudden fog over the face of the water. Ice-cold rain rushed down on us like a solid curtain. The whole world was expunged at a touch, and the sea was nothing save a foaming turmoil of rain-pitted water.

I buttoned my oilskin with a sense of satisfaction; I thought that we need not hesitate to get away now.

> *When the rain's before the wind,*
> *Halliards, sheets, and braces mind,*
> *When the wind's before the rain,*
> *Soon you may make sail again.*

The men of the old windjammers who made that rhyme knew their business. If you get the rain first, the wind may spring upon the ship all in a heap after it, and take the sticks out of her if she has not been snugged down. But when the wind has been raving for hours, as it had to-day, without one single drop of rain, then the rainstorm tells you that the real heart is likely to have gone out of the wind.

The owner's head appeared from the after-hatch.

"What about it?" he said. "We may as well drop down far enough to avoid drying out."

He was evidently of the same mind as myself; and the mooring buoy went overboard. We anchored before we reached Osea Island, taking our position carefully with the aid of the lead, in order to get a berth as close as possible to the edge of the mud on our weather side. It was almost dark now. The rain came in squalls only, but the wind as it whipped across my face was bitter. I wondered that the rain was not snow.

Still, I was singularly happy, I remember. I had expected that we should find ourselves in a comfortless berth (for any berth between Osea and Mersea would have been an abomination), whereas here we were in this snug little corner. As the tide fell, the sheltering mud would creep up quite close to us. Let the north-easter blow its bellyful now!

The creeks and saltings were about us, with the weird calls of the night birds, and the *wash-wash* of the dark water about the fringes. To me it is an enchantment always. I pushed off in the dinghy into the darkness, and paddled quietly up the little creeks. Miles of mud and saltings were about me, and the night was utter blackness itself, as of the pit. The little star of the bawley's riding light was a pin-prick of yellow in the dark landscape, and it was the only one.

Then again for contrast! As I came alongside, and hoisted myself on board, I saw small sparks blowing from the cabin chimney and an endless little trail of smoke eddying, and then whipped away by the wind into the night. Going below, I found the owner's coalfire glowing red, and the cabin flooded with yellow lamplight and genial warmth. I stretched out my legs in perfect luxury; here was homeliness and comfort indeed.

I slept like a top: the owner, sitting up in his bunk opposite, had been telling me some interesting details (about which I had asked him) when suddenly he found that he received no response. I was hard asleep already. I am sure that there was nothing but an amused smile on his face as he dowsed the cabin lamp and followed my example. I was conscious once or twice during the night of wind and sea; when the tide came up again, the bawley was throwing herself about in quite a lively fashion, but she was quieter in the grey dawn. When I poked my head out, there was a chill world of wind and rain, but we lay snug enough under the weather shore.

"Umph," said the owner as he joined me on deck. "It's going to be a dead-noser, and we'll have to use the engine if we want to save our tide."

The bawley had a regular fisherman's engine, one of those single-cylinder Kelvins. I had often heard the sound of them as they *chug-chug-chug* a fishing smack along, but I had never been shipmate with one before. The bawley had also a big capstan of modern design. To get your anchor, you turn the handle almost without effort, and up it comes.

From the Nass Beacon we should probably be able to fetch the Bench Head, so we made sail. And here let me say my little word about the bawley rig. I used to feel that it must be perfect heaven to have a mainsail without a boom while running, thus saving any anxiety as to a gybe. Don't you be too sure! The rig has its own drawbacks, both in running and beating; and my feeling now is that, whereas the ordinary risk in a gybe is that of carrying away a runner, your danger in a bawley is more serious and you may get your own skull cracked instead. The main-sheet is rove through one big block on the horse (and this block has a belaying pin stuck out on each side of it like a spike); there is another large block at the clew of the mainsail, and another still a little farther up the leach. I did not like those heavy johnnies slinging and cracking just about my head; they scared me!

There was an excellent case in point this very morning, as we made sail off Mersea Quarters. The bawley had been brought head to wind, and up went the mainsail, flapping and slatting and cracking as a sail does in a strong wind. The ordinary mainsail has its heavy boom which reduces the frolics of the sail; but the bawley sail has nothing to cramp its style. It is free to go perfectly mad, and to send those heavy blocks dancing in the air, just above the cockpit.

"There you are," smiled the owner, as we belayed the halliards and coiled them down, standing beside the mast. "You see, I can't go near the helm now without getting my head knocked off." He said it with a touch of indulgent triumph, like a man watching the frolics of a mettlesome thoroughbred.

In fact, we had to *crawl* aft; then the sail filled and went to sleep, and the little ship was slipping through the water.

At the Bench Head, course was changed for the Buxey Beacon. The tide was low, and this course would take us over the tail of the Knoll and right across to Bachelor Spit. The change of course brought the wind on to our quarter, and we carried on at speed.

"We shall probably touch," said the owner philosophically, "but I don't mind that."

In a Leigh bawley he need not mind; she is built for the job. She can bump on the hard shoals and take no harm. Like the Whitstable 'yawls' she can dry out in an exposed anchorage, and refloat safely under conditions of weather that would knock the bottom out of any ordinary yacht.

But she did not touch; the water calmed ominously for a time, and then again the waves began to be steep and foam-capped. We had crossed the Knoll and were in the deeper water again. Once more, the lumpy sea gave place to a dirty-coloured expanse of shoalwater, and then again came the lively steep waves of a tideway. We were across the Bachelor Spit and were bringing the Buxey Beacon abeam.

Now we had to gybe. And I, in my innocence and folly, had been accustomed to say that a gybe on a bawley is such a harmless affair! I did not altogether relish the 'harmless' prospect now, with that whipping mainsheet and those hefty blocks.

We had brought the Buxey Beacon abeam

"Mind the blocks don't brain you," the owner cheerfully enjoined, as he ducked down in the well, and I put the tiller up. I ducked mighty low as those blocks went over!

The Buxey Sands were partly uncovered, and the Foulness Sands over the bows were a dark line looking almost like a piece of coast. The Foulness Sands dry to a height of five feet five miles off shore, and they uncover almost as far out as the Whitaker Beacon. There were myriads of seabirds standing sentinel along the sands, or circling in great bevies above. The West Buxey Buoy was abeam and we were just approaching the Shore Ends.

Up Burnham River we scudded, and the whole world was sombre, under heavy skies. A sea-going tug was entering the river with us, and gradually she overhauled the bawley, while the latter at good speed in this smooth water was eating up the miles also. A yacht under full mainsail was preceding us; she would have been snugger with two reefs down. In every hard gust we came romping up towards her, for she had to luff and luff and luff. In the lulls she would draw away again; and we played this little game together all the way up the Crouch. The Roach was passed, and Burnham; and still the rain rained and the wind blew. At Fambridge we anchored, fourteen miles from the sea. We stripped off our oilskins and went below.

"Not at all a bad passage," I said, as I sat down at ease and stretched out my legs. "Stretched my legs," did I just say? No, I was wrong; I only *tried* to stretch them and brought up hard against the centreboard case. I was like Carruthers in *The Riddle of the Sands*, who had "not seen this devilish obstruction;" but there was less excuse for my blindness than for his. On board *Dulcibella* the centreboard case was hidden, beneath the table, "a long low triangle, running lengthways with the boat and dividing the naturally limited space into two." In the bawley, the case divided the cabin into two, and it was by no means beneath the table. It reared itself straight up through the middle of the table; and, with its chain and purchase, it was easily the most prominent feature in the whole cabin. It simply dominated the situation.

Did the owner care? Not he. He was not given up to chintzes and curtains, and the perfectly apt was to him the perfectly beautiful, either above deck or below.

This bawley is not everybody's boat; but her performance was certainly very efficient. As a strictly practical proposition, among the shoals of Thames Mouth she was *good*.

The Habit of Hibernating

O NLY THE FEW IT IS who keep their yachts fitted out all the year round. Speaking for myself, my own habit has always been to hibernate. It is not so much the cold as the long nights that deter one from winter week-ends. The cold was a factor all the same. True, the coal-fire in the cabin could make a prodigious fug in the evening and the early part of the night, but the penetrating chill of the small hours had to be experienced to be believed; it seemed to find its way even through a haystack of blankets. I dare say that an anthracite stove overcomes the night-chill; but anyway, as already suggested, it is not so much the cold as the dark that is the real enemy of winter cruising. Unless you can get the day off, you arrive on Saturday evening in the twilight. For these reasons, among others, I always laid up.

My shipmate and I, however, used in the old days to lay up only for a short winter. The shortest was when one year we laid up in early December and fitted

A great red ball of fire was over the Dengie Flats

out again early in the following March. But we *had* laid up. It was so well worth while, because the return to the waterside was such a thrill. We stood at the creek side again and surveyed the familiar scene; it had a new savour, a fresh charm. We went on board and heaved a sigh of content. The pause had done its work, having brought this fresh halo to the whole picture.

Colour was grey and dingy at the Burnham waterside one afternoon in March. The yacht was fitted out, and was already at her moorings; but the shore jobs seemed to be endless. Darkness was complete before my shipmate and I had finished them and were fairly on board, but we thrilled to the atmosphere of everything. The lamp-lit cabin was heaven, and the *lap-lap* and murmur of the tide against the hull was music of the spheres.

Blankets were inadequate that night, I remember, and the night was bitter. I was up at five in the dark to creep about the deck and to love it all, and at six I was off in the dinghy (while my companion still slept) to row round the yacht and feast my eyes on her. The rapture of it all!

Rain began. There was hardly any wind, and a pitiless rain all day. High-water would be soon after midday, and all that we could do was to beat up to Fambridge in the torrents. There we anchored and drank hot tea in the cabin while the rain swept pattering over the decks above. The day may have looked dreary enough to the casual beholder; to us it was a pure delight. The rain ceased in the evening, and the two of us sat on the cabin top in the darkness at the mooring at Burnham; we watched the lights reflected in the water and listened to the ripple of the tide. These things meant much to us after the hibernation.

Next week-end was better still. True, the Saturday evening was grey and overcast, but there was a decent sailing breeze. The mooring buoy was overboard at 5 p.m.; with a fair wind and a racing ebb we dropped down between the flat banks of the Crouch and were soon at sea. The old horizons, the old, well-loved wide expanse of treacherous shoal-sea! With the glasses I picked up each familiar buoy and beacon and claimed each as a long-lost friend. I can savour the joy of it still. The breeze freshened, and the clouds rolled clear of the sun, which was by this time setting—a great red ball of fire over the Dengie Flats. The distances were so cloudy that we were quite out of sight of land. In the twilight the seas were lumpy; they were breaking on the tail of the shoal as we scudded over, with little enough to spare, and darkness was upon us before we had gradually worked our way, on the wind, inshore towards the Bar buoy. Everything was a voyage of discovery and romance. In the lee of Mersea Island we anchored for a meal, and then we determined to sail over to the Bradwell shore and bring up there for the night. From the warmth and light of the cabin we turned out into a dark and breezy night. The yacht was rocking merrily. Side lights up, we reached down the Colne, keeping a smart look out for unlighted buoys, and then we turned to windward until we could get a sheltered berth close to the southern shore. At 3.30 a.m. we let go our anchor; and I lingered on deck before I turned in. It all seemed too incredibly good to be true—this space, this freedom, this dark, wind-streaked water, and, above all, this little wonderful yacht.

Each spring brings its own reawakening and pleasure; it never loses its zest.

From Mist to Sun and Wind

T HAT ALARM CLOCK WAS ALWAYS AN ABOMINATION, and never was the warmth and comfort of the bunk so great. A flash of the electric torch on to the clock's dial showed that it had done its work truly. According to plan, we had been awakened at 4 a.m. and in late September there is not a hint of dawn at that hour.

These early starts are all alike. Overnight it had seemed a capital idea, but in the chilly hours before sunrise, no. The bunk is desirable beyond words.

"Get the beastly lamp alight, anyway," croaked the voice from the opposite bunk. Then we did drag our unwilling limbs from bed, and we yawned and yawned. But in a few minutes we were jerseyed and sea-booted on deck, and one sluice of salt water had put us to rights.

"Glad we anchored at the creek-mouth," I said as I got down the riding light. "There's not much wind, and not a glimpse of dawn; it wouldn't be too easy getting out of the creek."

We were anchored in the Blackwater, off Bradwell in the county of Essex. We were bound for the Kent coast. If the yacht sailed away seaward without being picked up, she would find herself by sunset-time somewhere off Margate or the North Foreland. If, on the other hand, a slight mistake were made, here she would sit for the day, high upon the mud, a warning to all beholders, for the tide was ebbing.

The wind, though light, was unmistakable: a flat calm would have been a nuisance. But the dark was dark indeed: it was absolute.

"Got the traveller out? All right. Then we'll set the mains'l." The main halliards ran through the blocks and the noise seemed loud in the utter silence.

"Right oh," the sail was set. "We'll get the anchor now."

The lamp in the binnacle had been lighted, and we faded out of the creek: literally without a sound the yacht glided seaward with the faint breeze and the moving tide.

The object of real importance was the lighted circle of the compass card, which moved slightly this way and that, crossing and re-crossing the buffer's-line—just a little this way, and then back again. The breeze, light though it was,

The waters from Harwich to the North Foreland
"constitutes" the mouth of the Thames

was real—for the response to the helm was perfect. The yacht was making a sure course on her way to the Swin Spitway.

That course, though straightforward, was not direct, for the yacht's bowsprit pointed straight at the Nass and Mersea Quarters. By the lead, the rapid shoaling on the north side of the estuary would be our guide, and thence a straight line would lead us in turn to the Bench Head, Knoll and Wallet Spitway buoys.

"We shall see the Knoll light before dawn. The flash of Colne Point ought to be in sight now."

My shipmate scrambled off for'ard: he shielded his eyes as if to probe the dark. There was nothing: not a bead of light, not a glimpse, nothing at all.

Barely perceptible at first, dawn was beginning to filter gradually into the darkness. We could see one another now.

"Small wonder we couldn't spot the lights," my shipmate said as the grey dawn broadened. "There's a regular mist on the sea, despite this little breeze. No wonder!"

This mist was only a blurring of the horizons, but it shut off land and distant sea alike. By this time we must have cleared Sales Point and were in that system

41

of shoal-sea which is authentically Thames-mouth. The waters from Harwich to the North Foreland have been held by the Admiralty Court to 'constitute' the mouth of the Thames, and the definition is no arbitrary one. A glance at the chart shows that the whole region is one entity: the whole 'lay-out' of fairway and shoal is occasioned and conditioned by the set of the tidal streams in and out of the Thames; and our little Blackwater fairway was only one minor branch of the system.

Still we could see nothing. As for the yacht's position, we had not the smallest doubt about the line on which she was moving, for the cross-drift of the tide would be negligible; somewhere on a straight line drawn between the Nass and the Knoll buoy she was, but how far we had moved along that line we had no idea.

We began to fidget, for that question was rather important. If we didn't sail through the Spitway with the ebb, we should not get through at all. This feeble breeze would never push us over the flood.

Had we enough margin in hand? The blurred horizons gave no answer; we might be anywhere, and silently we sailed on.

'Knoll.' Yes, there it was, right over the bowsprit. It is always gratifying to see the shape of a buoy materialise just where it ought to be. The compass has a magic that never quite loses its wonder.

We had warmed our innards with a cup of tea before we left Bradwell, but now was the time for breakfast; my shipmate slipped down below, and I remained at the tiller.

Breakfast was finished before we sighted the Swin Spitway buoy; and we sighted it before we heard the distant sound of its clanging bell. This was worth a sigh of relief; we had saved our tide. We should be in the East Swin or Middle Deep before the flood of the tide, and that tide would carry us for six good hours London-ward.

And so it was. The wind was uncertain but sufficient, and the kindly flood tide, when it came, was certain and strong. Visibility was amazingly poor. We marked off our position on the chart, and leaned lazily in the cockpit. There was nothing in sight as we slid smoothly southward. Then one after another, after long intervals, fairway buoys came into sight; and, as we passed them, we watched the strong tide bickering and foaming past each buoy. Then the Maplin pile lighthouse (demolished now) suddenly took shape. The day was clearing. We could see the flat Foulness Island, and yachts in the Crouch—over the Foulness Sand. Was ever a passage so peaceful? The sun was breaking through, and the smooth grey water was gradually becoming a gentle blue.

"We shan't get across to the Kent shore before the tide turns again," one of us grumbled. "We shall miss the six hours of ebb down the Kentish Coast. We shall have to anchor."

As we spoke, the mainsail ceased to draw, and hung as limp as a shirt on the clothes line when a day is windless. The sun had dispelled the mist, and the air was warm; and so we drifted on. Noon was past, and it was nearly tea-time before we had brought the old Mouse Lightship abeam. That lightship, which used to show a flashing green light, is now no more.

Then at last came the real wind. The pale blue of the sea became a deeper blue, and the mirror-like water was rippled. This wind was easterly, and we set our course for the West Oaze buoy, beyond which was the island of Sheppey. A passage down the Kent Coast would now be a turn to windward. Everything was changed: the wind was soon quite vigorous, and the yacht was leaving a respectable wake of foaming white astern. This was splendid.

So the afternoon passed. It is odd how strong an east wind can be, in really fine weather with the glass high. When we were close-hauled and beating down the Four Fathoms Channel the spray was flying freely. We began to think of pulling down a reef, but it was not necessary as yet. We donned our oilskins, and we settled down to short tacks. Close-hauled we were thrashing through a very vigorous dark blue sea. Sometimes a curling wave would fairly hit the bows, and a sheet of sunlit foam raked the yacht. The salt spray on our oilskins would sometimes dry in the sunshine so rapidly that its little crust of salt glistened; then another shower came over and washed it out. The wind was even stronger now, and finally we did pull down a reef in the mainsail; and the yacht carried on just as well. Afternoon faded to evening and we were still turning to windward in short boards. The yacht was still toppling over the steep seas and was plunging into the trough, bowsprit under, when the warm sunlight had gone, and the blue water had turned to a grey-green sea. Without the sun the south-east wind was searching and bitter. Our hands were cold, and feet were getting a bit chilly also.

There is a curious sort of 'homeless' feeling when one has no certainty of a snug berth or a well-earned evening meal. One feels it most at dusk when the twinkling shore lights begin to shine like little pin-points, each with its suggestion of fireside and warmth and comfort. And now those lights began to twinkle on the Kent coast. I don't think that we were very forlorn on that particular nightfall—but this brought us to another topic.

Not so Easy to Stop

DOG-WEARY AT THE TILLER, many a yachtsman has felt that he would give worlds to be able to stop, and yet has been forced to go on, everlastingly, as it were. It is like Ixion on his wheel in Hades. Or as a more homely example, it is just like a learner on a bicycle. He is able to keep his balance as long as he can continue moving, but he knows that if he stops, he will be in worse condition. And so it was with us.

Night had fallen. The tide was running hard through the narrow gut south of the Hook Sands. The buoys, all unlighted, were becoming difficult to locate, and we were glad to have that great upstanding beacon (the Margate Hook) as an absolute guide. It gives the precise edge of the sand, and there are no awkward indentations to beware of. The sea was a riotous jobble of foam-capped waves.

"The trouble is…" I said, and then I paused for a moment as a briny stream shot over, "the trouble is that when we're round the Foreland, we shall have a contrary tide. And I don't fancy Ramsgate in the dark with a strong, onshore wind. Margate Harbour is dry already—drier than we are," I grinned as I ducked my head to take a regular cataract on the top of my sou'wester.

"Lee, ho!" It was about the tenth time in as many minutes, for the boards were very short between the sands just here. Far astern a few twinkling lights showed the position of Herne Bay; Reculver (invisible now) was abeam; and a few lights farther eastward on the low cliffs would be the lights of Birchington.

We had expected that the sea would be calmer as we closed the shore. With so much south in the wind it *ought* to.

The waves were less vicious and we could shake out that reef

The sea didn't do as it ought; it certainly did not. It kept on being as uncomfortably steep as ever.

"It would be against the grain too much to throw away all this windward work and go back to the Swale," my shipmate began. But I cut in. "With such a heavy lop of sea," I said, "I shouldn't care for a passage there at dead low water. There are very shallow patches on the Studhill and Clitehole Banks. Now we're through to the Gore we're safe enough from the shoals, and I'd rather stand off and on all night. I'd rather keep going all night than turn back, or than anchor in the foul discomfort of a seaway like this." He agreed, but the sea, a friendly element in so many of its moods, looked a dreary, foam-flecked waste in this late twilight.

Not so easy to stop. That was the bare truth. Could we gain a rest from our labours by lying hove-to? Certainly not. We had shoals under our lee, and the flood tide would soon be setting us strongly towards them. We had both been up since four a.m. but at nine p.m. we had no prospect of rest.

"Nothing else for it," I said, and I yawned. An hour passed, and we still buffeted along. But the waves were less vicious.

"Either it's the effect of the turn of the tide or... 'pon my soul, I believe we could shake out that reef."

It is wonderful how, at sea, one's problems solve themselves if one does not try to force the issue against the facts. The wind was steadying every moment, and before long the yacht's course was laid towards Epple Bay, a little indentation near Birchington, where we had lain more than once before. By midnight we were anchored. Stronger wind would awaken us, we knew; but the night was reasonably quiet, and we slept.

Early next morning we were away round the Foreland with the whole blessed daylight before us, and no need to think about 'stopping' for hours to come.

Tidal Islands

O N YET ANOTHER EVENING WE WERE TURNING through the Four Fathoms Channel, and we began talking about tidal islands. The wind was again easterly, and there was a bit of sea; but the evening was fine, and we felt confident that the breeze would take off at nightfall or soon after. Although, therefore, we had no sheltered anchorage in prospect, we were quite happy. The Four Fathoms Channel leads from the Nore right over the Cant, and lies south of the Spile and Middle Sands, and north of the Spaniard; it is so-called because it has a depth of four fathoms at high water. From the Mid Spaniard buoy we turned to windward across the Kentish Flats. At this state of tide there was plenty of water.

"Think of all the little islands drowned under this sea," I said, looking out across the blue seascape, lumpy and foam-capped in the low sunshine.

"Seen from the air, at low-tide springs, this place is a regular Archipelago," I added. A light spatter of spray came over the bows as I spoke, but the sea was good-tempered enough, and we did not need oilskins. All the same, it *was* sea; and it looked as open and shoal-free this evening as the Channel.

Some of the tidal islands of the East Coast that emerge at low water are said to have been real islands once. Look at the Buxey, off the mouth of the Crouch. They say that the name means Bucks' Island, and that the shoal was once an is-

At dead low water, we sailed the dinghy along to the Margate Hook Beacon and landed on the sands

land with green pastures and woods for the deer. At dead low water it is a flat level of brown sand now, and at high water it has gone.

"I never can resist an island," said my shipmate.

"Nor," I admitted, "can I. If I see an island, whether tidal or otherwise, my impulse is to land and explore."

Even on a map the same wizardry can get to work. I remember it from my early days at a dame-school. The geography books used to tell us that an island is a 'piece of land entirely surrounded by water.' And everyone in the class always knew the definition of an island, even if he did not know an isthmus. Why, even after school hours, I often stood gazing at the big roller map in the schoolroom, with wistful eyes upon those islands, entirely surrounded by the varnished blue that represented the sea. I tried to picture them; I longed to visit them.

A tidal island just crops up in the middle of the sea for an hour or so at low tide, and then disappears all the rest of the day. But, while it lasts, it is a stretch of honest sand or shingle, just like the solid foreshore.

The Goodwins are tidal islands on the large side. And what a grim place those Goodwins are! You feel the weirdness and desolation of them at its highest on some grey day when the long flat is utterly deserted save by the seagulls. For the time being the sands are an island indeed. Even if a gale of wind were raging, and the great breakers hurling themselves upon the fringes of the shoal, these hard sands would be a place of perfect safety for a mariner—*for an hour or so*. His ship might lie, broken-backed or sunk, under the pounding seas. Here, under his feet, the mariner would feel the solid shore.

It is a dreadful thing to think of, but it is said to have happened more than once. Seas have been too bad to allow of any boat approaching the sands, and watchers ashore have seen men on the Goodwins walking about. Nothing could save them; they were doomed. Defoe recorded a case somewhat of the same kind; but in that instance—contrary to expectation—the weather suddenly moderated and the men were saved.

We talked of this as the yacht turned to wind over the Kentish Flats. As we approached the West Last and the Woolpack, the sun was almost down.

"We've a good bit more of the ebb in hand," I said, "but I don't think we'd better go any farther. We can bring up somewhere here under the lee of the Margate and Hook Sands."

"Not too easy a berth if it blows in the night," my shipmate said.

"Small fear, I think," I replied. The glass was high, and there was no sign of mischief. *If*, of course, the wind breezed up too much, or we began to drag, we should have to get out. "There's the Girdler," I pointed, for the flashing light of the lightship was already visible. "We've got our position at a glance. But I'm not thinking of remote chances. I'm thinking mostly that the tide will be right down in the morning, and we shall be lying snug at breakfast time. That's much more important."

True enough, at breakfast time, we were lying there as snug as you please, and could have our meal in absolute peace. A light mist blurred the horizons and made them indefinite. The sea was calm, and sands were close aboard. Later on, at dead low water, we sailed the dinghy along to the Margate Hook beacon and landed on the sands. The sands were a firm island, with the sea about them on every side. Then, as the tide rose, we stood and watched it creep up the channels and thread along the little hollows in the 'ribbed sea sand.' Slowly the sea was covering our tidal island. Yard by yard it was dispossessing us of our narrow kingdom. Whether we liked it or not we had to go. And half an hour later our island was gone also.

'Ware Shoals!

E VERY TIME THAT A YACHT GOES AGROUND on a falling tide, that in-cident is really a rehearsal of shipwreck. There has been the lack of skill and foresight which may cause a skipper to lose his vessel. Upon place and weather the sequel will depend.

In a mud creek there is little harm to befall, which is a mercy for all of us. But even in the mud, piles and other nasty things may be sticking up, and the yacht will perhaps sit down on them as the tide leaves her. In that event there may be a rising bilge as the tide flows, or the yacht may be strained slightly over a large area, thus causing one of those infuriating invisible leaks that are well-nigh impossible to locate and get rid of.

In ninety-nine cases out of a hundred the mud is safe as houses, a soft and reliable cradle. But outside, on the hard sands and shoals, it is a very different matter. The yacht, for instance, that gets aground on the Shingles or the Gunfleet may never sail again. The elements of shipwreck are there all the time, and the skipper may pay the full penalty.

In these notes I have sometimes been an example of how not to do things. My worst achievement was to dry on the Pye Sand, but that was with a west wind when the shoal was under the lee of the land. And we have been very near to the full 'rehearsal of shipwreck' more than once.

We were beating out of the Crouch one nightfall when the wind was north-easterly (which can be a really dangerous wind there if it means business) and the weather was unsettled. The Buxey falls so steeply to the Ray Sand Channel that

49

Eternal vigilance is the price of safety at sea

it gives very short warning, however well the lead is plied. As a fisherman put it: "That sand, when it comes up, it comes up all at once." I was at the lead myself, the spring tide was tearing out seaward, and night had already fallen.

"Lee ho—quick!" I shouted urgently, for my last cast had shown that we had slightly overdone the board and were too close for comfort. I seized the long boat-hook and shoved her round to be quite certain, for the scend of the ebb tide is right across that shoal, and so will set a yacht upon it. The very feel of the iron-hard sand under the iron shoe of the boat-hook was grim; if she missed stays, what then? The sails filled away all right, but the incident remains indelibly in my memory. The recollection of the *click* of the boat-hook on the sand sets my teeth on edge at this minute.

Now suppose that we *had* really gone aground, what would have happened? The yacht was drawing four feet six of water, and the tide would have gone away and left her listing over on the hard sand. We should have got the longest rope we could muster, and have laid the kedge out where there would be deeper water when the tide made. We should have laid out the big anchor also. Then we should have sat there and waited, listening to the whine and whistle of the wind in the darkness, and we should have wondered all the time. We should have been very unhappy mariners, for this might mean the total loss of the vessel. Every sweep of the wind that seemed like a harder gust would have flayed our conscience as with a knife.

The weather was not rough when the big sailing ship Indian Chief ran aground on the Long Sand one dark night in the 'eighties.' But, as the flood made, the east wind was gradually sweeping up into a gale. The waves came up with the tide, breaking heavily; they swept and frothed over the sands in great combers. As the ship began to lift they pounded and thumped and banged her against that grim, unyielding sand. The ship broke her back and became a total wreck. The death-roll was heavy; and, had it not been for the supreme gallantry of the Ramsgate lifeboatmen, not a soul would have survived.

The skipper who puts his yacht ashore on a shoal has given hostages to fortune, and he must await her award. The award is freakish in the extreme. Some casual and self-confident fool, ignoring the counsel of his betters, will go aground, and fortune will send him a flat calm as the tide rises, so that his yacht will refloat without a scratch. Whereas the cautious mariner, overtaken, perhaps, by thick weather at nightfall, and getting aground by sheer ill-luck rather than folly—well, fortune may send a full gale to break his yacht to driftwood and very likely to send him to his own account as well.

One way of avoiding the rehearsal of shipwreck in shoal-waters is to treat a yacht as if she required about double her own draft and to lay course accordingly, just as if she were quite a big ship. This is not always possible, because some of the shoal passages are too useful to be denied; but, of course, in negotiating them, one is always specially on the *qui vive* and doubly careful.

There are other ways also in which shipwreck is rehearsed. Look, for instance, at the dragging of anchors. This may, or may not, be by the seaman's own default. I remember very clearly an occasion when the fault was mine. I had failed to moor properly; the yacht was lying to a single anchor, and I left her for a few hours. The wind in the interval hardened to a sudden gale, and the yacht was ashore (on the mud) before I returned. On the mud she was as right as rain, but suppose there had been hard shoals or open sea to leeward? Ship after ship, anchored in the Downs, used to drag her anchors and go aground on the Goodwins in just that fashion, so becoming a total wreck. A few years ago a yacht anchored in the Orwell dragged her anchors in a whole gale south-west by west, and was away to sea. She drove right out to the Shipwash, a dozen miles off-shore; and she would have been wrecked if the lifeboat had not found her just in time, and taken her in tow.

Eternal vigilance—it has been well said—is the price of safety at sea, and not under way only. Similar vigilance is necessary even when at anchor.

That Wretched Anchor

THEY SAY THAT A WATCHED KETTLE NEVER BOILS. And really one is almost led to believe that a watched anchor never drags. As long as watch is maintained the anchor, down there in the depths, seems to be conscious of its master's eye, and it keeps its fluke resolutely home, holding with a literal grasp of iron. I have stood in the well of the yacht, and taken shore-marks in alignment so as to be quite sure that the anchor was holding properly; I have stayed on deck a couple of hours or so, loafing and idling, and the yacht has not budged an inch. After that I have gone below just for half an hour for a bit of lunch, and then…

"Yes," the wiseacre will tell me, "you had only yourself to thank; you ought to have done"—this, that and the other. My answer to him is that I *do* make a point of doing this, that and the other, when I am bringing up for the night; but when I am merely waiting for a tide I don't; and nor does he. Some people in such cases lie to a kedge only, and there is no earthly reason in quiet weather why they should not. The bower anchor itself, however, is the very symbol and token of security. It is a low trick for the anchor suddenly to drag after it has held for a couple of hours, and when there has been no aggravation of wind or tide or increase of depth. But it sometimes does it—if one goes into the cabin.

I am not speaking of the cases when it was all one's own fault. When a man lets go with a short scope of chain on a rising tide, he need not wonder if his anchor drags; he has simply been asking for it. When equally, in a strong wind, he moors carelessly—throwing down his kedge anyhow so that it very likely first fouls itself at once with the anchor chain—well he, too, has asked for it, and he has no right to complain if he gets what is coming to him. Further, he is a public nuisance.

The wind blew great guns in the night

In Newtown River in the Isle of Wight some years ago (to quote an instance) I watched a biggish yawl bring up in precisely that way not far above me. The wind blew great guns in the night, and I spent an anxious time in my own well during the small hours watching her drag down as if she were coming right on top of me, while the people on board her were snoring comfortably below. I was positively in the act of getting under way myself (a cheerful business in pyjamas and oilskins), when I saw that she was going clear. I yelled, but got no answer; they were all still snoring, and she went on towards the open water outside. Finally, however, she brought up on the steep hard shingle at the entrance of the Creek, and took a heavy list as she dried out. Perhaps this list rolled some of those gross sleepers out of their bunks, and one rather hopes that they hit the cabin floor hard and truly. They deserved it. And they would only have had themselves to thank if the breaking waves or the heavy wash of some great passing liner had pounded the yacht on the stones so hard as to hole the hull and perhaps strain the timbers. They were not only incompetent, but criminally careless.

That sort of dragging is no wonder; the case is simply cause and effect, of offence and punishment. But let me give two instances where the watched anchor never dragged and the unwatched one was away at once. One day in the Medway we had brought up close to Chatham dockyard, and I had been sketching on deck for well over an hour. The yacht never budged one hand's breadth, so to speak. Then we went below for a cup of tea, and the next thing I was conscious of was the stone wall of Chatham dockyard a few yards outside the cabin portholes.

There was no engine to help one out in those days, and the job of getting sail on her was a hectic one, among a swarm of anchored craft. My shipmate and I were in an instant furiously busy at anchor and the halliards respectively, and I am glad to reflect that, though the yacht was within inches of another vessel, she actually got away without touching a thing.

But, most of all, I remember one day outside Poole Harbour. From the west we had sailed round Old Harry; we were rather weary after a passage, and anxious to get inside. The breeze which had been heading us had now fallen lighter, so that there was no chance of making Poole against the ebb. Again there was no engine to take the yacht scornfully over the contrary tide as it does now; we had to work our tides in those days every time. So down went the anchor. It was a glorious day now. Wind and tide were in the same direction, and therefore there was no chance of the yacht riding over her anchor. And the depth of water was decreasing. If once the anchor held, therefore, it ought with absolute certainty to hold, at least to low water, unless the wind breezed up. There was a good scope of chain. I sat for over two hours on deck, lazily watching the blue water and the dipping gulls. The entrance to Poole Harbour was quite close, and we could sail in as soon as ever the flood came along.

Then we went below for a spot of grub, and stretched ourselves out idly and chatted while we fed. The yacht hardly rolled at all in the light off-shore breeze. Finally, I looked up at the cabin clock, and said I thought that the tide would soon be on the turn now. We went on deck. Heavens above! The yacht had brought out Anvil Point clear of Old Harry, and we were well away to sea! The yacht must have started off as soon as we went below, and have gone like a train. Why? Can anyone tell me? Personally, I haven't the smallest idea.

The Suffolk Coast

HAVING AGREED OVERNIGHT to take full advantage of a favouring early tide, we turned out of the cabin, sleepy and unwilling, in the morning twilight, and grumbled and shivered, our hands frozen. From the warm bunk to the nip of the air at sunrise is not a happy change. We got the sails on her, broke out the anchor, and steered seaward. And, as the yacht settled down on her course, that old pleasure returned of sailing into the sunrise. The sea was still leaden in colour, with little foam-caps of a cold grey; but all along the horizon was the warm flush of the sunrise. The bowsprit lifted and dipped with a gentle heave, and the ripple of the bow-wave was crisp and business-like. Then, gradually out of the low-lying belt of cloud along the sealine, the red ball of the sun emerged, bit by bit. Another day had begun, and it looked like being a fine one.

The only drawback was the cold. Despite breakfast and hot tea and good woolly sweaters, our hands were wellnigh numb; so we donned oilskins to increase our animal heat. The ebb-tide of the Blackwater was racing out seaward, and we were sailing over the ground quite fast; at the same time the sun was gathering strength every minute. We swung our arms across our chests, beating them as the day-labourer does in frosty weather, and we really began to thaw.

As long as the tide was with us our rapid progress continued, but all too soon the flood began to check our speed, and the wind at the same time eased off quite a bit. The fact indeed must be confessed that it was six whole hours after we had broken our anchor that we contrived, at last, to reach the Rolling Ground and the coast of Suffolk.

The flowing tide streamed southward, and the wind was still light. But the sunshine was glorious. Those oilskins that we had used for warmth had been hung up long ago, and we were fairly basking in the blessed sunshine. With a fair wind one does not feel the breeze at all, and the sun was having it all his own way. The cabin-top was hot to one's hand, and we had fetched out cushions and were supremely idle. Under the sun the dancing glitter on the sea redoubled the sun's own effort, and landward the sea and sky alike were summer-blue. A perfect day.

My old shipmate has his own little way of talking nonsense: he talks it still, but he fairly bubbled with it in the years of our youth. I used to try to improve his mind by telling him of the old saws that I dug up about the Suffolk Coast and choice passages from old books that I happened on. There was, for example, Drayton's appreciation in 1613 of Orwell Haven:

> *For Orwell comming in from Ipswitch thinks that shee*
> *Should stand for it with Stour, and lastly they agree...*

Besides of all the Roads and Havens of the East,
This Harbour where they meet is reckoned for the best.

His only comment, of course, was that 'beast' and not 'best' is a rhyme to 'East,' and that this upsets the whole apple-cart of the silly poem, and he didn't think much of these 'poet fellows' anyway.

And now, to-day, we were sailing past the Cork light-vessel, with a light breeze and brilliant sunshine. Away there on the low coastline now was Felixstowe, which looks nothing but a modern seaside town, but really is of great antiquity, having been the 'stowe' or dwelling of Felix of Burgundy some thousand years ago. The place was recorded in the Domesday Book as "Fylchistowe or Fylstow." Beyond it, basking in sunshine, was Bawdsey Cliff and the little haven beside it. That entry can be very dangerous, with its shifting shingle banks and swift-running stream; in the ordinary way it is wise for the visitor to signal for the pilot. We used to do so as a rule, but on a gracious day like this we should probably have had a cut at it ourselves, with a rising tide and a quiet sea. Once inside, it is very snug, with good holding ground; and Deben river, leading up to Woodbridge, is delightful. Woodbridge "was richer than Yarmouth and all its members combined" in the reign of James I, a flourishing port for foreign trade, and building its own ships. Its old glory has departed long years ago.

We were steering now for Orfordness; the coastline north of the seamark on Bawdsey Cliff falls gradually away to the levels of the long shingle bank which runs on to the Ness. In the curve of the bay are Shinglestreet and Orford Haven; and if you can spot a cluster of small houses, a Martello tower, and coastguard station all close together, there is the mouth of the Ore. The position of the entrance, like that at Bawdsey, is always shifting (it is said to have been at one time a mile and a half from its present position); the tidal streams run very fast, and the shingle banks will not hold an anchor. We always had a great respect for the terrors of this entrance, and we always signalled for the pilot.

Both of these bar harbours (Orford and Bawdsey) are believed to have been much easier and deeper in the Middle Ages. But all of that has long gone by. Suffolk seaboard is indeed a very chain of ancient seaports which have ceased to be. Wadgate Haven, Walton Castle, Goseford, Orford, Thorpe, Sizewell, Mins-

Off Orfordness we had an easy passage

mere, Easton, and Dunwich have either disappeared or have ceased to be serious seaports at all.

With our fair wind we were slipping easily through the blue water, and our content was complete; we were crossing Hollesley Bay, which used to be a favoured anchorage.

We had by this time brought Orfordness abeam, and we sailed close inshore. Old Grenville Collins (in 1692) further said: "You may sail from Hoseley Bay down to the Ness all along the Beach, having good sounding;" it still holds good, and so—close inshore—we sailed. Sunshine was still brilliant, and over a summer sea we looked at the tall lighthouse tower, bright against a clear blue sky. Such passages as this have no incidents; they provide little to record, but they are the very essence of a lazy and peaceful passage. If such days as this were of very frequent occurrence, they might become tedious; but as things are, along our home seaways, they are real jewels—a perfect joy. So we sailed on. The lighthouse on the flat yellow shinglebank was now fading astern, and—with a bubbling white wake following our counter—we were leaving it dwindling into the past.

Landward of the Aldeburgh Ridge shoal we hugged the shore, and were soon off Aldeburgh town; a stone's throw from the shinglebank over there was the River Ore—invisible, of course, from the sea, but authentically there. More than once we have landed in the dinghy and have stood on that narrow neck of shingle between river and sea; river and sea are only apart by a matter of yards, but the passage by sail or power from Aldeburgh river to Aldeburgh seafront would be some two and twenty miles.

And so, in the afternoon, we continued our idyllic passage, warm and genial in the westering sunshine. Southwold was now in sight, its lighthouse on the cliff in the town, and the pleasant sands dotted with groups of sun-worshippers, basking as idly as our own selves. In passing the harbour I called to mind our anxieties and tribulations when we had to coax the yacht as best we could between the twin piers, with a strong tide sweeping through the open piles, athwart the fairway. The harbour piles would cut off the best of the wind, and we made feverish efforts with sweep and boathook; or there was furious towage from the dinghy—unless, of course, we were lucky enough to be able to pass a warp to men on the pier who would haul her in. All of that 'trouble, fury and sweat' is obviated by the engine: you come in at your will and all is well if you can find a berth. With two warps run out to the harbour wall, and anchor and kedge out in the stream, the yacht lies snug beside the wall, allowance being made for the rise and fall of the tide.

In the prevailing south-westerly winds, the breeze is comfortably on the quarter all along this coast from Orfordness to Yarmouth, and one has an easy passage. Even in a really strong sou'wester, no weather eye need be lifting to avoid an unexpected gybe, nor is there that slewing, this way and that, which one knows so well on the foam-topped following seas, when running free.

White cloud had sailed across the blue during the day, but all cloud was disappearing now, and, in sunshine slanting toward evening, we sailed in a golden glow. Kessingland and Pakefield were discernible, and Lowestoft was in sight. The River Waveney, which enters the sea at Lowestoft, is a narrow stream now, but it was once a broad tidal estuary.

Tired and happy, we entered Lowestoft Harbour, and tied up in the tier—a snug berth which gave us a night of unbroken sleep.

"Them Barnacles"

CRABS HAVE A LIKING FOR BARNACLES. The name 'barnacles' does not refer to those long stalky creatures which foul the bottoms of deep-water vessels; it refers to those limpet-like shell-fish that are a perpetual nuisance to the yachtsman. Their attentions vary with time and place. Sometimes the yacht seems to keep clean for several weeks, and sometimes the space of a week or two is sufficient to produce a fat crop.

However that may be, it is a part of our modest life afloat to get the little ship from time to time up on the scrubbing hard, and to shred off those beastly 'barnacles.' I made my discoveries about the crab's love for them many years ago when I did my scraping in shallow water as the tide receded. The moment the scraped barnacles began to fall into the puddles, all the water was simply alive with crabs innumerable, scuttling after the choice morsels. Crabs are grotesque things to watch, and perhaps—in the hot sunlight—one paused from labour a little more than was needful. Pauses from work, none the less, are needful enough. The attitude when one tries to scrape the keel, *and cannot kneel to it* is no fun. A complaining back has to be straightened out. In my seaboots I splashed to and fro; and I crushed any number of crabs. I could not help it.

And it was amusing to see the crabs at work, and how they handled their food. The bigger ones squatted on their haunches and fed themselves comfortably, taking their food in their claws, first one and then the other, and popping it into their mouths. But what really annoyed them was the idea that smaller crabs were getting a good feed too. That they couldn't stick at all. They would drop all their loot to chivvy after some young spark who had got a bit for himself. And the young one ran for his life. All this did not tend to work.

It is surprising what a difference a scrub makes to a yacht. With the old straight-stemmer in particular a clean hull is highly important. Otherwise she is apt to be uncertain in stays. She goes about in a long curve in the ordinary way,

"It ain't the ship's fault," he said; "look at them barnacles!"

the wind being out of her sails for a good part of it. Her momentum carries her round, but she needs to go through the water as clean as a whistle. Those little limpets are like the teeth of a saw, checking her way. And if they check it beyond a certain point she misses stays—more especially if she has been sailed too fine.

We knew all this for a fact, but it was brought home to us in strong terms some many years back. Returning, after absence, to the yacht in the Deben, we found that she had just begun to grow a beard—a modest beginning, but a beginning all the same. I was in a hurry to get back to the home mooring, and we made sail at once, bound seaward and home. If sailed ramping full at the end of each tack, she was perfectly confident. It was blowing hard, and we had pulled two reefs down. The bar of Woodbridge Haven was a small lather of foam, and we took on the pilot to see the yacht out. We warned him, as he took the helm, that she was very slow in stays. With the weight of the pilot's heavy boat in tow, she was likely to be doubly so. I told him that, too. I was perfectly game to take the helm myself, but he preferred to do so. We were away.

At Woodbridge Haven, as everyone who has entered knows, there is a long shingle bank, half submerged, opposite the shore, and shoals from the shoreward side go out to meet it, leaving a very narrow passage (with 3 ft. at l.w.s.) for navigation. In a strong south-west wind the waves break on the bank, and any ship driven ashore would break up—unless a power vessel could tow her off at once. Anchors are useless in that loose shingle.

"She ain't going to miss? Gord, she ain't?"

Fear, entreaty, and impotence were mingled in the pilot's voice as the yacht— with that lee shore right beside her—trembled in the wind. If ever I heard dismay in a man's voice it was then.

"Them Barnacles"

I do not know to this moment how I managed to streak along the length of the yacht at the speed that I did. And it was only afterwards I discovered how badly I had barked my shin in doing it. Anyhow, I had contrived to fling myself for'ard just in time to hold the shivering foresail out as far as arm would reach to windward, clinging on meanwhile for dear life to the stay with the other hand. The backed sail took her off the bank; she filled away and was safe.

Once clear of the bar, we made a board shoreward and put the pilot off into his boat under lee of the land.

He stood in his boat and shook his fist at the yacht.

"She's a — " he shouted.

I should be sorry to repeat the word he used. Not only was it most improper, but it was rather silly. No yacht on earth could possibly be what he said that yacht was.

Then, as the old yacht lay down to it, her weather side exposed, he diverted the attack to ourselves. His voice, half lost in the wind, was audible still:

"It ain't the little ship's fault," he yelled; "look at them barnacles!"

Despite 'them barnacles,' she never once faltered in stays in a prolonged and dirty passage home. But, once home, it was not many days before she was put on the hard for a scrub. 'Them barnacles' might have cost her her life.

Behind the Shinglebank

Y EARS AGO, BEFORE WE HAD EVER ENTERED the River Ore at Orford
Haven, I had put my eye (when looking at the chart) on that big tidal lake up
beyond Aldeburgh. We thought we would like to explore it. We did explore it, but
not quite in the way that we had intended.

The yacht had been lying off Shotley in the River Orwell, so snugly under the
weather shore that one did not realise the strength of the wind. None the less, my
shipmate and I pulled one reef down when we made sail. The yacht streaked down
the Orwell in the finest possible style, past the Bell buoy, the breeze coming fresh
and strong as we opened the Stour. We had soon rounded Landguard Point and
were at sea, the wind on our quarter as we laid our course for the Cork Light Vessel.
I have forgotten what little thing was amiss up for'ard, but I went along to settle it,
having asked my shipmate at the helm to luff up a moment for me. The moment
he did so a great wave broke over the bow, wetting me with spray from the waist
downward and putting water into my sea-boots. I was not in oilskins. It would be
a bit lively if we had to turn to windward; but our wind was free for Orford Haven.

Away we went, with the wind dead aft as soon as we were on our true course.
And as the yacht was sheering so wildly we stood offshore on 'port-gybe,' and
then back inshore again on starboard, aiming at where we believed the harbour
entrance ought to be, though there was no smallest sign of any inlet on the whole
stretch of surf-fringed shingle. The book of the words told us to look for a "bay
with boats afloat in it." No part of the coast looked more bay-like than any other,
and there were no boats; that was certain. We looked rather blankly at each other.
"They've pulled the boats ashore on account of the weather," said my shipmate.
"And anyway," he added dolefully, "I don't suppose the pilot would put off to us
on a day like this."

We had already hung an oilskin on the rigging, this being a recognised signal.
I also was very uneasy, but we decided that we could close the shore a good deal
more, and then — if there were no activity betokening a pilot — we should still have
tons of room to stand out again and run for Lowestoft. The shore, with that surf on
it, looked wicked. "I am afraid we must…" I was beginning, when, even as I spoke, I
spied a small boat under a reefed lug-sail, pitching jauntily over the waves and send-

The wind was on our quarter as we passed the Cork Light Vessel

ing the spray flying in sheets. Down came her sail, and the mast was unstepped. We steered down upon the boat, hoping to goodness that it contained the pilot, and not a couple of fellows come out to fish or something. No, it was all right. Clearly they were intent on us. In a splendid curve the yacht swept round, and as she luffed up beside the boat one of the men sprang on board. "Not a very nice morning you've chosen to come up," he said, and he took the helm. "What do you draw?"

"Three foot six."

He nodded and steered straight in. "There's not a lot of water on the bar," he said, "but she won't hurt."

Not even a semblance of a break in the shingle was yet visible, though we could now see the leading marks. The waves were breaking heavily on the shore. If the yacht went aground she would be an utter wreck. The kedge might be laid out, but it would only come home at once through that loose shingle; and each wave would crack and crack the yacht still harder on to those mounded knolls of shingle. I was glad that this imperturbable fellow was at the helm, and not I.

63

Then all of a sudden the miracle happened. It appeared an utter miracle to us, who had never entered before. One of the great shinglebanks seemed to heap itself up on our beam, and we were conscious of shelter. That great bulwark of shingle that had seemed to stretch unbroken from Bawdsey to Orfordness was not as continuous as it looked. There was a hole in it.

And here was a river, and a barge stolidly loading shingle in smooth water, a beach with boats on it, and there were cottages; and—the sea had gone. It was a marvellous transformation. We were inside. The pilot took his seven-and-six-pence and dropped back into his boat.

We had bags of time in hand, bound as we were for Aldeburgh, and so we got the mainsail off her. It would be much snugger sailing under headsails only. And the contrast of that quiet passage remains in my memory to this day. The smooth water and the gliding movement, between the shinglebanks at first and then be-tween fields, and past the ancient town of Orford. All the time the tall lighthouse on Orfordness was visible, and once or twice I swarmed up the mast and looked (across the narrow tongue of land) at the sea outside. For six or seven miles the river runs parallel to the sea.

That night we lay snugly in the river of Aldeburgh; and on the following morning we decided—according to plan—to explore the tidal lake, the 'great salt lake' as we called it in our talk. The wind demanded two reefs. After a mile or so of sailing up the river we were in the open 'broad.' The tidal flats were only partly covered, and the channel was thus declared. Easy job this. But in the meantime the tide rose.

Sailing westward it had been necessary to beat. With the lead kept going we were warned each time we were inclined to leave the appointed channel, and we went about and stood over until we received similar warning on the farther side; and so on.

And then we went about, to return to Aldeburgh. We were now off the wind, and the yacht flew. She flew in what I faithfully believed to be the true course. Withies or booms were merely conspicuous by their absence; there were none. And the tide had risen; it was getting on for high water now.

"I wish to goodness we'd turned back earlier," I said anxiously. "It won't do at all to go aground at this state of tide." And, on the word, she brought up.

Fairly and truly, she had sailed on to the soft mud. She stopped and the dinghy came up and hit her.

Down came the sails, and I was in the dinghy in a moment and away, sounding with an oar to locate the true channel. "Here we are," I said. "I'll lay out the kedge and we'll soon be off."

Lay out the kedge I did, and it came home precisely as if it were coming through butter. Not even a check; not the smallest effort to hold. I tried again. Same result. The mud was some of the blackest and filthiest of ooze that even a connoisseur like myself had experienced. My hands and clothing reeked of it as I tried and tried again. No good.

"We've only a very small margin of tide," I said at last, "and unless we can coax her off under sail she won't come at all." I left the kedge and warp and all their filth in the dinghy so as not to defile the yacht, and I fastened a tow-rope to the bitt-heads to try to pull her head round. I might as well have pulled at St. Paul's Cathedral; she not only wouldn't budge, but there was not even a vestige of 'give' about her; she was fast.

"Nothing for it but to get some ballast out, or we're here for the night." We broke up the floorboards and began a bit of ballast-shifting. With labour we transferred one or two pigs to the dinghy, and the filthy warp and kedge were distributing their contributions over the clothing of both of us all the time. And the stuff stank.

"Another shot now," I said, and my tone was colourless and utterly bereft of hope. We settled to the oars and—at the first stroke—she came. Not after a vasty effort, not grudgingly, but instantly and all at once. She floated as if she had never been stuck at all.

We made sail; and, with amazing luck, we made good our departure from that 'great salt lake' without further incident; and once at anchor again at Aldeburgh we scoured and cleansed every last vestige of that black mud off warp and kedge and dinghy. Our own clothes took a bit more cleaning still.

It had been amazing luck. We had got off well after the time of high water. Whether the tide was late or there was a special little freak of Providence in our favour I cannot say. The day remains 'a memory of mud.'

Britannia in the Nineteen-Twenties

B RITANNIA, THE MOST FAMOUS YACHT IN THE WORLD, was still wearing her old gaff sail-plan in the nineteen-twenties. New rigs were given her in 1921, 1926 and 1927, but not until 1931 did she come out as a Bermudian. In 1926 I was privileged to be a guest in her, in the first race of the year. This was at Harwich regatta, and her competitors in the big class were *Shamrock* and *White Heather*. This was not my first race in her: Sir Philip Hunloke (he was Major Hunloke then) had been a good friend. Needless to say, a guest like myself had to doff the apparel used in the mud game before going aboard on the King's yacht, and to dress properly.

The June morning was sunny, and here we were. The order to the crew is crisp. "Come on, me lads, let's have the tops'l up!"

Harwich Harbour, dotted over with white sails, lies blue in the sunshine, and the King's splendid cutter is away. The sunshine is hot; almost over-hot, perhaps, for it may eat up the breeze. The breeze is southerly and none too certain. *Shamrock* and *White Heather* are busy; the white-clad crews of them, white dots along the decks, make little hives of industry.

"Got your compass-courses? It may be thick."

Yes, the bank of low cloud seaward looks suspiciously like sea fog, but there is more body now in the breeze, which has shifted easterly. It will be a reach out of the harbour, and then a long turn to windward, out to the Rough.

"Clear over the jib; break out y'r stays'l."

She will soon be in full trim now. Working jib tops'l will suffice for today, and up it goes, in stops. "Watch y'r jib tops'l sheet," calls the skipper; "don't break it out."

Odd it is how the angle of vision has suddenly narrowed. Earlier this very morning, every yacht afloat in the harbour had been a source of interest. The tall *Norada*, gracious-lined, the staunch yawls *Rendezvous* and *Sumurun*, and the whole fleet of the twelve-metres—all of these, and many others, were filling the eye. They are still there, no doubt, busy on their own concerns, but the only things seen and felt now are *Shamrock* and *White Heather*, rivals for the line. They are watched closely as any cat would watch a mouse. "That's his game," says someone, "sail off on starboard tack"; "No," is the next guess, "he's off after the other fellow. Chasing him." Someone else confirms it; and then—with a white puff of smoke—goes the first gun.

It is a pity that *Susanne* could not start, and that *Westward* and *Lulworth* are not entered, but the elements of a sterling race are here, none the less. We shall see.

The second gun follows, and the three yachts are away, over the line, in a bunch. *Shamrock* and *White Heather* are on equal terms, and *Britannia* just astern of them. The first race of the season has begun.

"Stays'l sheet! Jib sheet in!" The white figures have jumped to it. "That'll do y'r jib! *Stays'l!*" And the three yachts are fore-reaching together, swiftly down the harbour to the Cliff Foot Buoy and the open sea. *Britannia*, on *Shamrock*'s quarter, cannot luff more on account of the shoal-water to windward; she might, if she would, call for water, but she prefers for the present to drop into *Shamrock*'s wake. "Come more to loo'ard, boys," is the word to the crew. "Not too much. In the middle of her." So, in close order, the three tall yachts sweep seawards.

On the wind now, they are beating for the Rough. *Shamrock* is on *Britannia*'s beam; her glossy topsides are so pure and polished as to reflect her own bow-wave in perfect detail, clear as in any mirror.

"Now then, boys, put her about. Handle her smart." It is the skipper's voice as Major Hunloke gives him the word and puts down the helm. Smart it is, and she has settled to the new track.

The breeze is coming to life, and *Shamrock*'s big jib-topsail is rather more than she needs. Down it comes by the run, and the men are busy on her bowsprit, bundling it in and setting the 'baby.'

At the Cork Light Vessel, *White Heather* has established a lead, and *Britannia* and *Shamrock* are crossing one another on short boards. Up comes *Shamrock* on starboard tack, and Major Hunloke—not electing to shorten his own board— bears away with instant precision. Judged to an inch is the clearance; and *Britannia*'s bowsprit—after seeming to rake the whole broadside of her rival—shoots past the green stern of her, clear. It is brisk work.

No further tack will be needed, and the three yachts will now fetch the Rough on a long leg; they are pointed at it on a compass course, for the buoy is a mere dot, as yet unseen, somewhere on the blue sea-line.

Past the Rough, the course is for the S.W. Bawdsey Buoy, and *Britannia*, by holding longer to her old tack than the two others, obtains the windward station. She is beginning to rebel against third place. Her moment is coming. The water is bubbling away astern of her in spate; she is dropping hawk-like on the buoy.

The wind will be dead aft from the S.W. Bawdsey home. Out mainsheet now! The wind has fallen lighter, and the crew are hastening the main boom out with arm and shoulder.

"Come on, me lads, square away that spinnaker boom!" The spinnaker is set, and everyone is aft in the sunshine while the three yachts settle to the long run. So dead aft is the wind that *White Heather* is on the opposite gybe to the other two.

As is usual in running, the wind seems to have gone utterly. With the hot sun and the easy movement there is a sense of drowsiness; it is an indolent luxury to slide over the blue sea in perfect sunshine. Major Hunloke, for a breathing-space, relinquishes the wheel to the skipper, and looks round at his rivals—running free, one on each side of *Britannia*. "Well," he comments, "a one-design class couldn't be much closer than the three of us are to-day."

Literal fact it is; for, after twenty miles of sailing, it would be well nigh possible to throw the proverbial biscuit on to the deck of either yacht. It is anybody's race.

So the three cutters spill the sea-miles astern of them, running free. They sweep on, their white wakes in parallel. *White Heather* decides she must be on the same gybe as the others; over goes her mains'l to starboard, and she crosses the track of *Britannia* out towards *Shamrock*, where *Shamrock* is holding an unbroken course for the Cork, with the white water streaming by, into the long wake astern of her.

Then, like a thunderclap on a day of cloudless calm, comes the sudden jar of surprise. Every figure on each of the yachts is electrified into instant attention. Coming up through her lee, *White Heather* has luffed *Shamrock* with an amazing suddenness; the manoeuvre had been looked for by nobody. *Shamrock*, swift in her reply, is luffed also, curving from the bowsprit that assails her; she is clear. But no. As ill-luck will have it, the wind has played traitor or the high gods have not approved. Her luck is out. Within a hair's breadth of being clear, she has been just touched. A sporting rival is sadly and almost unaccountably out of the race. For *Shamrock*, her topsails handed and her staysail furled, is soon headed for home, and the race is poorer for loss of her.

But the manoeuvre which has cost *Shamrock* her race has cost *White Heather* her pride of place as well. She is no longer leader by a whole minute and a half, as at the Rough. It is now neck and neck for the Dovercourt mark-boat. Down upon it the two yachts converge: *Britannia* may not have the lead, but—on the inner station—she will have an overlap at least, and *White Heather* must give her room. Which yacht will it be? Come now, settle down and watch; it is worth watching.

Then the twelve-metres, all in a bunch, materialise out of nowhere, and bid fair to complicate matters. But they somehow fade out of the picture again; and the two tall yachts—each intent on the other—race for the mark.

"It'll be a sharp gybe. Lookout for your runners!"

The pace is headlong, as can be seen when the Cork Light Vessel seems to sweep by at a run. And this is the very spice of racing—this handling of a yacht with instant energy, with headlong eagerness. The skipper looks to his crew. "I shall want that spinnaker in, pretty smart," he says, at a nod from Major Hunloke. Then it will be all hands on the mainsheet, of course, and pretty sharp about it.

The mark-boat with its blue ensign has sprung into shape and size beside *Britannia*. "Come on, me lads, now play smart," is the word. And the trained crew of *Britannia* jump to it as one man. The water boils under her forefoot as she rounds to the wind, and heels, settling down to it, while she drives arrow-straight for the harbour. And where now is *White Heather*?

White Heather is in the white wake of *Britannia*! *Britannia* leads! *Britannia* leads, and up the harbour the two of them race. At the mark-boat is a smaller yacht, rounding also, and it is sharp work for everybody. But *Britannia* has snatched a lead of three-quarters of a minute from her rival on the first round. And what now of the second?

Out again seaward the two of them romp, *Britannia* showing the way. *White Heather* tries luffing inshore to win an overlap. Bearing away, she romps down on the Beach End Buoy, and shoots up again for the windward station. She has shot too far and is all a-shaking. No; she cannot manage it; *Britannia* leads her still.

It is the windward game once more. *Britannia* is about.

"All full up for'ard there?"

"All full, sir."

Spinnaker to starboard; Britannia is leading

But *White Heather* is sailing like a witch. She means to have the wind of *Britannia*. The royal cutter makes short boards to checkmate her, but *White Heather* is not easily gainsaid. Handled—as she is—with perfect sympathy and skill, she is a sight for sore eyes, that fleet white cutter in the sunshine, as she slips through the sea. Tack for tack the two yachts are sailing; but *White Heather* has contrived to seize the initiative, and to put *Britannia* on her defence. She tries to catch her on port tack, and *Britannia* can barely evade her. To and fro they slip, speedy, though the wind be never so light.

She has done it! Up romps the white yacht on starboard tack, and *Britannia* must give way. But she will not sacrifice an inch. Holding on to the last instant,

Major Hunloke bears up. The skipper's willing hands are with his own on the wheel, forcing the spokes over at speed. But *Britannia*'s bowsprit *will* hit her, at the shrouds... the runner... the crash must come! No. The bowsprit swerves harmlessly past her stern, with scarcely a foot to spare, beautifully judged.

The short boards (turning for the Cork) are telling against *Britannia*. She is quick enough in stays, but she does not 'get going' quite so fast on the new tack; she does not 'pick up' with equal speed. Give her longer boards and she will whittle away the short lead which *White Heather* has now established. Give her a good puff of faithful breeze, and she will do more.

White Heather seems to have got well away. The Cork Light Vessel is now far astern, and *Britannia* is slowly retrieving her lost place—just a little. Nevertheless, she cannot come up with her comely rival, who is by this time right away at the Rough, a full minute ahead, and the two cutters—in all their grace—slip onward through the sunbright afternoon for the S.W. Bawdsey.

But the wind is now very light, and this windward work in light airs is *White Heather*'s own; *Britannia*, even with her new rig, is not so responsive to this mere whisper of wind. The prospect for the race begins to look a little bleak, for—at the S.W. Bawdsey—*White Heather* has established a lead of a full three minutes; and only the short run home remains. She looks like an easy winner.

Round the buoy she sweeps, and is away for home, spinnaker to port. The climax of the race has been reached at this buoy; unperceived at the moment, here the fate of the race is to be written. *Britannia* is also at the buoy. "Unhook your lee runner"; here we are. And Major Hunloke has reached the decision. Clear and decisive it comes:

"Spinnaker to *starboard*!"

With swift energy the thing is done. But there are dubious faces on *Britannia*, and heads are shaken. The wind is dead aft, and there is not much in it either way; but is she not slightly by the lee? The spinnaker is drawing—the whole sail is one great splendid curve—bellied out balloon-wise; but the main? It hangs in creases, no willing curves about it. The pity of it, if *Britannia* is on the wrong gybe!

And the wind—trivial before—gets lighter and lighter. Faces lengthen, perhaps, and the cheery confidence becomes a little hollow. Well, well; never mind. She has rendered a good account of herself; with her old rig, she could never have done this. *White Heather* would have left her almost out of sight in these gentle breezes. *Britannia* has done well; there will be no runaway win against her to-day.

But no race is over until after the gun, and eyes are eagerly computing the sea-space. It is true! *Britannia* is closing up the distance. Sure and unswerving as Fate she must look from the deck of *White Heather*, as she comes silently on, on, on. The advance is imperceptibly gradual; it is slow but absolute, it is silent but inexorable. On, on, on. She is closing up; she will soon have *White Heather* on her beam.

There is no doubt of the proper gybe now; *Britannia* is right; and *White Heather* is well aware of it; *White Heather* must gybe. She has handed her spinnaker already, and, as her main-boom swings over, *Britannia*, with her whole spread of canvas full and drawing, has proudly swept by her. It is a marvellous moment; the royal cutter is a thing of pride and splendour. *White Heather* astern of her, setting no spinnaker for the short run that remains to the Dovercourt mark-boat, looks shorn of her full glory, reduced, downcast, outsailed.

A fresher puff of wind comes opportunely now, giving a vigorous finish. Round the Dovercourt mark-boat the two yachts sweep. Mainsheets are hauled home, and the yachts heel from the breeze, racing up the harbour with a world of white water astern of them. It is *Britannia*'s race; she is cheered from the small boats lower in the harbour, and caps are waved for a King's win. Faint cheers reach her from the distant shore, across the blue water. On, on, on she drives, with *White Heather* somewhere in her wake. Gun! She is home! And it is a full eleven minutes later before *White Heather* has followed her across the line.

*   *   *

"Rather a *lucky* win," Major Hunloke said afterwards. In sober fact, it was nothing of the sort. The thing was decided—as already mentioned—at the S.W. Bawdsey Buoy, by his own judgment. Had he followed the leading vessel (always an easy thing to do) he would have sailed on the same gybe as he did, and did rightly, on the first round. But, since then, there had been a slight shift of wind. This factor was, as it happened, a vital one; he sized up the situation with more decision and accuracy than his rival, and this it was which won the race for *Britannia*.

A Night Out

THIS WAS A NIGHT PASSAGE OF A MINOR SORT, but it was one of those unrehearsed effects which so often live in memory much more than a passage undertaken with due forethought. It just happened. We have often crossed the Thames Estuary by night, but I do not remember one occasion on which I enjoyed the crossing as much as on this one.

We had sailed up-Channel with a fair wind, and had brought up in the Downs the night before. We slept late because we had had a longish passage, and felt that we were now practically home. And when we did turn out in a brilliant world of sunshine, the tide was contrary and the wind light. The yacht was rocking gently, and the sun-dazzle on the water made one feel drowsy, even after having slept the clock round. We looked across at the sunlit white cliffs of Old Parker's Cap, and at the yellow shingle bank outstretched away towards Deal, and we yawned and did nothing. A lazy day.

Not until the early afternoon did the wind begin to breeze up a little. Still in the southwest, it was soon quite a vigorous draught. Though off-shore, it put life into the sea at once, and little foam-caps showed on the waves. We should have an excellent reach as far as the North Foreland, but after that there would be—as usual—a turn to windward up to the Nore, where we intended to anchor, and to take a few hours' sleep.

Deal Pier was soon left astern, and we shaped course inside the Brake Shoal, by way of the Ramsgate Channel. This saves a little distance as against the Gull Stream, and it affords smoother water. Old Parker's Cap, 'on' with the end of Deal Pier astern, is the leading mark which carries one right through the narrow fairway between shoal and shoal. On our port hand stretched the wide opening of Pegwell Bay, behind which lies Sandwich; and over the bowsprit was Ramsgate. The stone piers of the harbour were soon brought abeam, and we were sailing beside the low chalk cliffs that continue to the North Foreland. This fine breeze was splendid, and despite the contrary tide we reached past the Broadstairs Knoll buoy at speed. Clear of the Foreland itself, we opened the Thames Estuary, and had hauled in our mainsheet and were away for Princes Channel. The Tongue Light Vessel was visible on the horizon; we were in Thames-Mouth once more.

Then, on a lee-going tide, we began the everlasting game of to-and-fro. "Never mind," we said, "the tide will soon be turning, and we will work up to the Nore, and then let go and turn in."

The sun was well down towards sunset, and was shining full in our eyes. We were in the tracks of the shipping here; a big ocean freighter and a timber ship with a deck cargo were shaping course London-ward, and a topsail schooner was away seaward with a fine wind. She passed us at close quarters; with every sail set and drawing, she looked a picture.

We were in no hurry, and were perfectly happy. Later on the tide came to our aid, but the breeze fell lighter. There is a great impression of space and distance when the sea is smooth on this busy world of shipways. The flatness of the water gives the sense of space, and the shipping dotted about all round the horizon, dwindling objects with little smudges of steamer-smoke, convey the impression of distance. By the time we had brought the Girdler abeam the tide was doing most of the work; the wind was bone-idle. Not that it had deserted us entirely, for we still left a little bubbly wake in the smooth blue water. A tanker came astern of us, slid by and was soon little more than a blur on the western horizon.

By the time we had entered the Oaze Deep, the fact had become clear that— unless the wind came to life again—we should be nowhere near the Nore by the turn of the tide. What should we do? We were bound for the Blackwater, and there was no virtue in making the Nore. We could, of course, work in over the Cant and let go there, out of the tracks of the shipping. The sun was almost setting in a sort of golden haze, and the evening was perfect. Why not let the ebb take us and drift us on homeward? A short-lived draught of light breeze settled the question; we were able to work the yacht across decisively towards the Mouse shoal, along which the ebb would run north-east towards the Barrow and Black Deeps and not due east back to Princes Channel.

We had an evening meal, leaving the yacht more or less to her own devices, for she was now as idle as a painted ship upon a painted ocean. And after that, we thought we would watch exactly what she did. If she seemed inclined to drift in any direction where the shoal water was too shallow for our fancy, we could always bring-to. A great red moon was just peering over the eastern horizon. Really this *was* a wonder world just now.

We reached past the Broadstairs Knoll buoy at speed

The ebb was beginning to take her. It might drift her back to the Girdler yet. We therefore made every effort to keep her under control, working all the time towards the desired direction. The moonlight on the water was like molten silver, and the shafts of light from lightship and lighted buoy were blinking and glittering all round the horizon. One of them in fact blinked a good deal too close for comfort later in the night; it seemed as if the tide was drifting us right down upon the buoy, and we discussed whether we would do a bit of towage with the dinghy. We decided not. It is no easy task to decide in which direction to try to coax a yacht, and the mariner can quite easily find that his fevered labours have drawn her into the line of tide that will drift her on to the buoy instead of away from it. In the event she cleared it by an ample margin.

The wind quickened again before we had reached the mid-Barrow Light Vessel. The sail through the quiet moonlit water was a perfect dream, we seemed simply gliding in space. All the time we had been checking our course carefully by means of cross bearings between lights, and had marked down continually our position on the chart. And we were glad that the breeze

75

had come to life, for the one thing we did not want, here in the tracks of the shipping, was mist.

The eastern horizon was at last palely blue. Dawn. The low sky gradually warmed in colour, and day was beginning. From the Barrow Deep Light Vessel we shaped course by compass for the Swin Spitway, but then the wind again forsook us, and we had to anchor in order to avoid being carried too far to the eastward by the ebb. The sun was just peering over the horizon when—having set the alarm clock—we turned in for a five-hour sleep. Though peaceful and entirely uneventful, it had been a memorable night.

A Terror by Night

IN THE CABIN OF A LARGE AND SUMPTUOUS YACHT, when all were chatting in a group after lunch, I noticed that a retired admiral pricked up his ears at some idle word that I had let fall. I had spoken of unlighted buoys. He joined our corner of the group, and nodded acquiescence.

"Do you know Malta?" he asked me later. I had to confess that I did not; and, in my turn, I listened with interest to a tale of the iniquities of that terror by night—the unlighted buoy. In the Mediterranean, as on the coasts of England, the unlighted buoy can evidently be a source of worry and fret, even to sailors who are not of the amateur variety, and to ships that are not under mere sail.

True, if 'the mariner' were able to lay an ideally true course 'clear of all dangers' (as the Admiralty phrase is), he ought to have no fear of spoiling his topsides or smashing his bowsprit on any buoy, however invisible. With a power-boat it is infinitely simpler; and, in our own home waters, where the proportion of lighted buoys is so high, the thing can be brought off with comparative certainty under power. But where lights are not lavish, the problem—even under power—may become an anxious one; and, in home waters under sail— well, my shipmate and I have had our bad moments.

The Thames Estuary, more prolific in buoys perhaps than any other part of the watery world, is apt to present this problem—sometimes when one least expects it. Sailing by night, one thinks one has provided against every contingency;

then comes a shift of wind, which means a turn to windward instead of a reach; or the wind breezes up in such strong earnest that one's whole navigation becomes a bit breathless and wobbly.

That last admission sounds bad. But even a scientific navigator, when he has to turn to windward among the Thames shoal waters on a dirty night, while the rain and spray make a dark blur of everything, and the yacht is jumping and pounding all the time—well even he can get a bit shaky on his bearings. For our own part, we have trusted to rule-of-thumb methods in shoal waters, just as the fishermen do.

As we all know, the fair wind that has given us a fast passage up-Channel and through the Downs means a turn to windward after the North Foreland is passed. With a south-westerly wind, a fine long-leg can be made by way of Prince's Channel, and the wind only draws dead ahead in the Oaze Deep. The fairways are so well marked with lighted buoys that the passage presents no difficulty, even at night, in the ordinary way.

When, however, the wind sweeps up really strong, bringing rain as well as a heavy lop, the difference is astonishing.

"Yes," a friend of mine told me, "we were so blind with the rain and spray, and so shaken up and jolted by the sharp pitching, that we simply—well, we felt simply lost; the compass unsteady, and not a blessed thing to be seen except a very occasional stab of light, just a pinpoint here and there—always in a different place; beyond that—nothing. We trusted to the steamers. 'For God's sake,' I said to old Smith, who was with me, 'for God's sake hang on to that steamer's stern light as long as ever you can keep her in sight; and after that, with luck, we'll pick up another. If we don't, Heaven only knows where we'll bring up in the end; I don't.' "

They got through, as most of us do somehow. Then there was another well-known small-boat sailor, who some years ago published an account of how he was nearly wrecked on the Gunfleet Sands, and how he sent up flares which no one saw, although the pile lighthouse was well within sight. He also got through in the end. But these things show how difficult even experienced men can find things.

Very well. Do not think, then, that the picture is overdrawn if anyone says that, once or twice in his own recollection, unlighted buoys have been a veritable

All buoys, unlighted or not, are a blessing by day

terror by night. All buoys, unlighted or not, are a blessing by day. But slashing along close-hauled on a dirty night, it would be a hideous knock if you fairly got an unlighted buoy head-on.

"Keep a bright look-out," says you. You try it. The look-out from a steamer's bridge, high above the spray, has a chance; but on a small yacht, no. You may start your trick with a certain degree of confidence, but it will not last long. You button tight the collar of your oilskin and pull your sou'wester down over your ears, and then you lay for'ard, as desired. You 'lay for'ard' much more literally than the merchant crew does, for you have to lie full length to be able to peer under the stays'l. Wallop! The yacht hits a steep sea, and you are smothered in water. You clear your eyes of it and peer again. With the sharp lift and dip of the yacht you can keep no sense of any horizon. There is nothing but a great blur of darkness, which begins to fizz and froth in your eyes with the glimmers of foam-edges that drift this way and that, during the intervals when your eyes are not bunged up with salt water.

Beating in from the Barrow Deep I remember being in dread of the Heaps, the N.E. Middle, and the S. Buxey. Another night the West Swin and the Maplin Edge kept us on tenterhooks in the same way. But we never saw any of them. Another night it was one of the Margate buoys; and that one we *did* see. We were slashing along, close-hauled, to close the shore for shelter. The look-out, blind with rain and spray, had capitulated, and come aft. It was useless.

"Great Heavens!" he suddenly shouted. "What's that?"

Only the fringe of white foam had disclosed it, close on our quarter. A toppling black object dropped away into our wake. It was the S.E. Margate.

"My hat!" said my shipmate, "I never want to be nearer than that!" And nor, I confess, do I.

Tom Tiddler's Ground

TO THE SCHOOLBOY A PROHIBITION is often an invitation. The thing is forbidden, and therefore must be done.

Nelson, as a schoolboy, was an example. There were some fine pears growing in the schoolmaster's garden, which were naturally regarded as lawful booty—being so obviously and ten-times-over forbidden. But the boys dared not take them. Horatio Nelson, therefore, volunteered; he was lowered down at night from the bedroom window by some sheets, plundered the tree, was drawn up with the pears, and then distributed them among his schoolfellows, without reserving any for himself.

"The child is father of the man;" and so the same impulses remain. For this reason it is that many of us in our time have desired to sail just where we shouldn't. The very fact that a locality is all shoal makes one cast covetous eyes at it; forbidden pastures always look green, and the coast beyond the shoals looks well worth closer inspection.

A friend of mine who once lived at Whitstable told me that he so much wanted to sail beyond the ordinary limitations that he built a little shallow-draft yacht for the very purpose. His first appearance in her was little short of a triumph. She stood close inshore into quite impossible waters. Never having seen her before,

We worked inshore near the old Maplin Pile Lighthouse

the whole waterside population took her for a stranger that had gone *Astray* and would soon 'larn better.' But she skimmed here and there in perfect freedom. On the Whitstable yawls, men paused, dredge in hand, to watch her, and the shore-side loafers took the pipes out of their mouths to point her out. The Street itself didn't stop her. "Where the blazes has the little goddam thing come from, and how many bally inches of a rain-puddle o' water does she want to swim in? Gosh. She's a winner!"

It was quite a triumph. My friend played the whole afternoon upon Tom Tiddler's ground and was never caught once.

The appeal of Tom Tiddler's ground is, first, that you ought not to be there, and, secondly, that you get it in the neck if captured. And my shipmate and I, in the old days, would plead guilty to many minor excursions in that direction. And the same motive was there one day when we found ourselves in the Swin, during the early evening, with a strong south-westerly wind knocking up an awkward and uncomfortable sea. The water was—by contrast—smooth over the Maplin Sands, out of the run of the tide. We had often before looked across at that broad province, which was, of necessity, 'off the map' except at top of the tide. But now we had a light-draft vessel. The wind was cold, and we were tired. I was not certain (and am not certain to this day) whether the prohibition to 'anchor or ground' on the Maplin Sands applies northward of the notice buoy. Anyway, we decided to bring up. The tides were neap, and we worked inshore somewhere between the old Maplin Pile Lighthouse and the Fisherman's Head. When, by the lead, we computed that we should just float at dead low water, we let go. Even if the wind were strong the yacht would be unlikely to bump, because there would be no heavy lop until the water were deep enough to keep us well afloat, and thus unlikely to touch the bottom when dropping into the trough.

So, upon Tom Tiddler's ground, we spent our night. And we slept like a top. I was not conscious of any undue liveliness in the yacht's behaviour, although the wind was vigorous, and the Swin itself was probably a turmoil of breaking waves.

Next day I told a fisherman that we had brought up near the Maplin Light the night before. He, of course, imagined us lying—miles off shore—at edge of the fairway. He took his pipe out of his mouth and grinned, showing a fine row of white teeth. "I allow you didn't lie too snug, not there?"

On the contrary, I do not suppose that I ever lay snugger.

PART II

Down Channel

Panorama

I N THE NURSERIES OF YEARS AGO a panorama was a joy. It consisted of a picture of immense length, on rollers, which was displayed, a little bit at a time, through a wooden frame. As you turned the rollers new beauties and wonders were disclosed; and wherever you stopped there was still a complete picture, for the whole thing was continuous. A wonder, truly! It was one immense picture all the way, and yet it was always different, always changing.

Along our own coastlines a real panorama of supreme quality is always available. In far-away seas John Masefield could say:

> *I have seen strange lands from under*
> *The arched white sails of ships.*

And even to us stay-at-homes much the same sort of panorama is possible.

In a little voyage from London to Southampton, or from Weymouth to Falmouth, the coastal panorama is of amazing diversity. It runs on continuously, and any section taken (like the section in the wooden frame) is a thing of interest and beauty.

That is where the little coastal cruiser scores. The deep-sea man lays his course well out to sea, and the shore line, if visible at all, is only a low streak on the horizon. Look at the illustrations in the Admiralty pilot books—those long profiles of coast. The profiles are panoramas truly; but they are on so small a scale that—from the pictorial point of view—they simply do not count; even the boldest coast becomes tame and insignificant. And precisely the same holds good in reality.

The man who wants to make a good passage, or wants to sail right into the blue, is a fine fellow, but there is another type of passage to be had; and when we are sailing for pleasure (as we all are) it is often well worth while making the very most of the panorama. On a passage, my shipmate and I have passed Beachy Head at dawn, ten miles out, when the headland—low on the horizon—looked no more imposing than a long spit of sandhills. And we have passed it, close inshore when it towered above us in sunlight in almost fabulous splendour; or at dusk, a marvellous bastion, heaven-high. The low Suffolk coast, from a few miles at sea,

Beachy Head towered above us in the sunlight

is a mere nothing; close at hand, with its low cliffs, little woods, and square-tow-ered churches, it is delightful. And down West the headlands like the Dodman, from five miles offshore, are insignificant; close at hand they are superbly bold and craggy.

In fact the value of the coastal panorama varies in inverse ratio to the distance. Is it not so?

And there is another panorama as one gets older: the panorama of memory. We look back with pleasure to the past days of sun and storm. For myself, an old shipmate is a figure in almost all of those days, both in cruises when he sailed with me in my yachts, and I sailed in his. In later days he adopted the Bermudian rig, but I did not. I made enquiries, but—finding that, when the mast was stepped farther aft (as would be essential), it would spoil the cabin—I remained a back number. Together we look back at the old yachts we have sailed together.

To the Isle of Wight

WE WERE LEAVING LONDON RIVER and had sailed with a fair wind down the Princes Channel. Then, with a beam wind, we reached from the Tongue to the North Foreland, after which we had to work to windward, with a long and short leg. This was a grey day, the clouds were sullen and the sea was a greenish

A peaceful picture it was as we reached Dungeness

grey. The wind was fresh, but the yacht was keeping the sea in its place; there was none of that cutting spray which is so usual with a sou'wester wind. All the same we were rather glum. We were bound for the Isle of Wight, and it looked as if we were to have a foul wind all our passage. The south-west wind is so persistent. We had a fleeting thought of bringing up in Ramsgate harbour; but the tide was favourable, and the glass was steady. Through the Gull Stream we made our passage to the Gull L.V., and carried on close-hauled to the Downs and Deal. In the late twilight we had made good our passage to Old Stairs Bay, and there we 'let go.' The wind was taking off, and we had anchored here before. The glass was now rising.

We were on deck again at sunrise and, marvel of marvels, the breeze was a fair wind! The quiet north-east wind, which veered to the south-east, was a gift from heaven. In highest spirits we got the sails on her, and we were away. The sun was rising; and yonder, over a pale blue sea, the perpendicular white cliffs of the South Foreland stood, magnificent in the level sunlight. The South Goodwin Light Vessel was visible far away and was now astern; and we were shaping our course for

Dover. We have encountered some roughish seas here in our time as well as these halcyon conditions. When last we were here the fishing smacks thrashed through the foam-capped seas. To-day, past the detached mole, the yacht skimmed over this peaceful sea, and the coastline was falling away towards Folkestone and the broken slopes of the Warren. The ripple at the bows was delightful; the wind had more body now, and the dinghy was splashing merrily in tow. Far away on the horizon was the lighthouse of Dungeness, rising solitary out of the sea—for the promontory itself was still below the blue sea-line.

A peaceful picture it was as we gradually approached that flat shinglebank. This insignificant bank, which at its highest part is only some 4 ft. above the level of high-water springs, has been advancing seaward for years and years. While the seas have been corroding and washing away (for example) the earth cliffs of the Suffolk coast, and many other places likewise, this bank of loose pebbles resists the full force of the south-westerly gales that come roaring up the Channel, and indeed turns to the attack, moving seaward. By Trinity House observations this promontory appears to have been advancing seawards for the last century and a half pretty consistently. Eight or nine feet per annum has been about the average speed of this seaward march.

We were sailing well, but the wind was now too light for a fast passage. But very happy we were to enjoy this azure sea and cloudless sky. Off Dungeness was a usual cruising ground for the London pilots; and the old pilot schooners were very picturesque. They used to lie week about in Dover Harbour and week about cruising off Dungeness.

The breeze was again freshening a little, and we were slipping along nicely. The tall lighthouse was abeam, and we were soon crossing Rye Bay. Fairlight Cliffs in the distance, earth-coloured, were bright in the sunshine. Smacks were standing close inshore, and were evidently returning home to Rye. Our orthodox compass course would have been for Beachy Head, but we preferred to watch the panorama of the coastline. A topsail three-mast schooner (and it is a joy nowadays to see them with their old grey or tanned sails) was shaping course for Beachy Head, and we diverged more and more. Fairlight Church, a regular sea-mark, was visible, and on we sailed past Ecclesbourne Glen and we were off Hastings. Five and twenty years ago the Hastings smacks were all under sail; now they are

We had passed Dover Harbour

engine driven, and as a rule set only their mizen sails. Nevertheless they keep the old mainsails on board, in case of breakdown. A couple of these bluff-bowed shore-boats passed us close at hand, but *chug-chugging* under power of course. They are still picturesque.

After Hastings the coast for a time is rather insignificant, and therefore we did now steer for Beachy Head. That long chalk headland, and the range of downs stretching away landward, was a long ribbon along the horizon. And so the afternoon went by. We sailed shoreward of the Royal Sovereign Light Vessel, with the sun in our eyes, and we were off the headland as the evening set in. The tide had turned against us, and we were afraid that the wind might fail us at nightfall, but no; it held. In the night there could be no object in following the coast; we did hug the shore as long as the tide stream continued to be against us, but then it was a matter of a compass course for the Owers. "Happy is the Country that has no history," and happy were we to have no history during this summer night. The wind still held, and at 4 a.m. we had sighted the Owers light. We then changed course to leave the Light Vessel some two miles on our port side, and steered for the Nab. The dark water bubbled and rippled past, and the foam spread off in long ridges into the dark astern. And so came the dawn. The stars above us had disappeared; the water around us reflected the luminous warmth of the sky to the east. The breeze was still fresh. By day the Isle of Wight would have been in sight, but in this early dawn it was lost in a grey haze. But the light on the Nab was stabbing the twilight, and made the course easy. It was broad daylight long before we made good the passage to the Island, and we let go the anchor off St. Helens. This was a perfect summer day; we had never before had a passage so peaceful.

The Sudden Intruder

H OW WELL WE ALL KNOW HIM—the Sudden Intruder! The whole haven will be as quiet as the grave until the moment when one really wants it clear (in order to have plenty of space for manoeuvre in getting away), and then, and only then, in comes the Sudden Intruder, who seems to buzz all round the place like a fly round a honeypot.

We had sailed one day down the Solent and into Newtown River; and then we had brought up quietly in what we conceived to be a well-selected berth. At dead low water there is not overmuch space. Newtown River is an admirable little estuary, but the natural anchorage is rather over-monopolised by private moorings. Near the mouth are oyster grounds, and a notice board is exhibited ashore inviting you to anchor higher up. Higher up are those moorings and the tidal mud; so you can take your choice. Our own choice had led us to anchor well down, by Clamerkin Lake, close enough in to be clear of the fairway, but not so close in as to take the bottom at low water. We had kept the lead going when about to bring up, and we took another sounding when the yacht was finally riding to her anchor. All was well.

This being so, we were surprised to get a polite message from the oyster fishery asking us to shift farther out from the shore, as we should ground upon the oyster beds. We did not argue the point; it is always best to be amenable and accommodating, and to avoid all appearance of evil. So we broke out the kedge, and put it in the dinghy with a long warp, and began the little job of shifting.

No one other yacht had stirred in the harbour before that moment, and no yacht stirred for the rest of the evening—save during the few minutes that immediately followed. Precisely at that moment itself—yes, here he was, of course, punctual to the minute—the Sudden Intruder!

We had sailed into Newtown River and had brought up quietly in a well-selected berth

He was in a small yacht, using his auxiliary engine. A hand for'ard stood ready with the anchor.

"Yes, that's all right; let go here!" called the skipper.

It would be far from 'all right;' it would give us a foul berth in our new abode, and we warned him accordingly. He went off like a Christian; which goes to show that, once he has discharged his evil mission, the Sudden Intruder ceases to be inspired of the devil.

The wind breezed up hard in the night or early morning, and we were on deck, in a dour grey dawn, pulling down a couple of reefs in the mainsail.

"It's one comfort," I said to my shipmate, "that we're away so early, when no one else will be stirring."

The tide was rather low, and the banks uncovered; we were glad, therefore, of space enough to get away comfortably. Getting under way from a mooring one can always coax the yacht to fill on the desired tack; but when the anchor is hove in short she may insist on filling away on the wrong board. And unless the hand at the helm is quick in stopping her (at which even an experienced hand may fail) the anchor will be broken out before you can say Jack Robinson.

My shipmate was at the tiller, and I was busy up for'ard. I had been shortening and stowing the chain. It is a busy moment. The anchor must be stowed, the sails sheeted home, and enough way got on the yacht to go about with certainty before she is foul of the next yacht.

To my amazement and horror, at this instant I saw a motor boat close aboard of us and the skipper in the act of letting go his anchor at the very spot where we must bear away after shooting into the wind at the end of our first board. The Sudden Intruder right enough— here he was!

"If you let go there I shall be on top of you!" I roared in a voice of such volume and fury as to surprise even myself. The Intruder's engine was still ticking over, and he rushed aft and got the boat going again. What next he reckoned to do thereafter I don't know. He steered to and fro; mostly, it seemed to me, trying to get under my bowsprit, and he finished up by going aground.

Where *had* he sprung from at that hour of the morning, and with a riding light still alight, though he was under way? Evidently he had been anchored somewhere outside, where he had lain snug enough in the quiet evening; but, then, unable to endure the discomfort of the stiff wind that had sprung up, he had cut and run for it, without even troubling to douse his riding light.

The Sudden Intruder is no myth. Everyone knows him.

The Cruising Spirit

TO MY SHAME AND SORROW I OWN IT; I do not possess the full and true cruising spirit. That lot cannot be the lot of everyone, and I am one of the poor specimens; I am simply not in it with some men I know, as regards that placid and adaptable frame of mind which is the true fruit of the cruising spirit.

It is not that I have found myself wanting in times of stress or trouble. Even among the poorest of us such a failing is seldom encountered; and I, like all the rest, have generally muddled through somehow. But my inferiority comes out even there; for I do it with the utmost expenditure possible of nerve-strain and foreboding. Until things are *really* bad I spend my imagination in thinking out, and providing escape from, all sorts of awkward predicaments which may never happen. I believe a good many other people do the same, though they do not always own up. And I believe that they also, like me, only become reasonably placid and contented when the awkward predicament has really arisen. Then the fight against odds brings its own inspiration, making a man even of the abject.

I am not thinking, however, of that aspect of matters just now—but of the ordinary everyday cruising outlook. I was shamed into realisation of these things the other day when, lying in a mud-berth in my yacht (not yet fitted out), I heard a song as glad as that of a skylark. It was some fellow singing; he may not have had high musical proficiency—on that point I am not competent to speak—but for sheer joyousness and freedom I have seldom heard his music matched. It had the merry note that only a man who is happy to the core can put into a song.

And guess where my songster was! Thigh-booted, he was knee-deep in the mud. On Easter Monday he was shovelling the mud away from the keel of his yacht which, had she only floated from her winter berth (as, by all the rules of the game, she ought to have done) would have taken him for his projected Easter cruise to the Channel Islands. The spring tides on the South Coast since January had all been short; even the March tides, usually bumper ones, had failed to float his vessel. He had lost his Easter cruise, and was spending his holiday digging out his yacht instead. Grumble? Not he. Every time you met him his happiness was infectious and did you good. At low-water he was digging, and at high-water he was on deck with marlinspike and knife, hard at work at rigging jobs which he had intended to carry through in mid-channel on his cruise.

The poet says

Had Fate
Made me as hapless, I had been as great.

Speaking for myself, I am sure that I shouldn't have been. I should have groused. I should have been telling people about it all and expecting their sympathy. But *he* had the cruising spirit to its uttermost, and the chances of the game were all one to him.

He came on board me for a yarn once or twice, at intervals between his la-bours. I mentioned Newtown River, I remember; and he smiled reminiscently.

"What was it?"I asked.

"A double casualty," he laughed. "I was in a 24-tonner, and there isn't much room, as you know. But I had brought up in a snug berth, making myself a nuisance to nobody—unless perhaps the oyster people. And I was rather pleased. Then another pilot-cutter of about my own tonnage came in, and—went bang aground."

He paused. Good Samaritan as he was, I might have known that he went to the rescue. So he did.

"I thought I could fetch him off with my auxiliary," he went on, "but I couldn't." He paused. "The fact is I went aground myself on the other side, and we both dried out. Drawing seven foot six we both lay over at a mighty angle, so that, while some of the berths on board were quite comfortable, the ones oppo-site—weren't!" "So your week-end was spoiled?" I hazarded.

"Not a bit," he answered. "We found all sorts of things to do. We made a great bonfire ashore, for one thing, I remember. I daresay I never enjoyed a week-end better in my life."

There you have it; the genuine article. That is the spirit.

Yet once again, a week or two after, I heard that cheery note of song. The neaped yacht was afloat by now, and she came proudly in from sea. Her sails were soon off her. A kedge was down as well as the big anchor, and some pulley-hauly was in progress to the merry tune of a shanty. The same note of utter happiness was in his voice. Then my hero came ashore, and I noticed that the bridge of his nose was gashed and his nose itself newly blooded.

"What on earth—?" I asked.

"Oh, the block of the tops'l halliard fell on it," he explained. "When did it happen?" I asked.

"Just this minute, as I was getting the tops'l off her," he laughed. And he went striding off, the happiest man you ever met.

Her Sore Offences

A SMALL BARGE YACHT HAS HER GREAT and Christian virtues; in her own waters she is often of immense merit. But she has also her own little ways, which may be amusing enough in their particular line, but they do not always strike one as funny—at the time.

My old *Growler* was built by John Howard, of Maldon, and is probably the prettiest thing of her kind he ever produced. Good though she is, I must recall a couple of incidents in which she left me, if not irate, at least pained—and humble. And both times (for truth will out) she had me aground.

She will not bring off those two tricks again—not if I know it. Every day of my first year the old dear found that she would have to get up yet earlier in the morning every time she wanted to get to windward of me. And long now we have settled down to a sort of mutual respect—each with a watchful eye on the other, but quite happy together. True, she has her own back a bit in a rough seaway; that long rudder of hers, with its shallow draught, gets half out of water; and, when the next wave covers it, the tiller kicks like a horse—nearly knocking one over. I think she grins every time she gets me fairly in the ribs.

And now as to those escapades. I should like to ask anyone who has been accustomed to deep-keeled yachts what he would do if, running free down Beaulieu River, he wanted to gybe at the Needs Oar corner. Would he not haul in his mainsheet, adjust his runners, and put up his helm? Of course. And he gets his mainsheet nicely home before he belays, in order that the *jerk* when the boom flops over may be as slight as possible. A keeled yacht understands him perfectly when he treats her like that, and plays up. A barge does not; she stops to argue. "You're contradicting yourself," says she. "When you haul in your sheet, you want to luff; when you put up your helm, you want to bear away. You can't have it both ways." And that was exactly what *Growler* said on this occasion. She hovered for one moment, and then made up her mind. "I believe in sails more than rudders," she shouted, "and *luff* it is!"

In sober fact, I am only recording what actually happened at Needs Oar. There was not time or room for me to circumvent her sudden plunge before it was too late. With her helm hard up she put me ashore to windward. She sailed in the ex-

The last turn in the Channel before Porchester was our undoing

act opposite direction to that which the helm ordained. The tide was falling, and she sat on the edge of the mud and winked at me. "Now you know more about barges than you knew yesterday," said she.

I did; and, as I say, she will not bring that trick off on me again. I have learned her little ways; and, after all, one can see the explanation of that escapade. Her lateral hold in the water is so slight.

The explanation of her next achievement may be less obvious to the lay mind, but the moral is clear. I knew beforehand that I must not press a barge when turning to windward, but I did not know that I must be even more careful not to over-canvas her when running free. I learned it at Portsmouth.

We had been bound for the harbour in a strong wind which would be fair for me at the entrance. *Growler* could just stand up to the wind on the reach, and so I had no fear of it on the run. But the moment we made the entrance I found she was partly out of control. She would luff out at a touch, but no persuasion on earth would make her bear away one inch. She made a rake's progress of it up

Portsmouth Harbour, for the wind suddenly sprang into force and volume, and fairly bellowed. I was anxious, but fairly confident. If we gave ourselves room to luff before reaching any unavoidable obstruction we should be safe. If we made Porchester Channel it would be a matter of luffing gradually all the way.

She went like a train; she fairly streaked through the harbour, and I thought we should bring up at Porchester triumphant, without having had to reduce canvas.

But we didn't. The last turn in the Channel before Porchester was our undoing. The tide was still very low, and the turn in the Channel required me to bear away. I might have got through if I had taken a fifty-fifty chance of hitting a post. But I was out for Safety First. The post was hard and the mud was soft, and I luffed the yacht and put her aground. An hour later she was anchored safely at Porchester. She had not winked at me that time; she knew I had acted wisely, and she looked at me with some respect and a little contrition. "Pretty well judged," I might have heard her mutter.

These are her two sore offences. I will tell also of her virtues (and they are many). But, in the meantime, I suggest two morals. When you want to gybe a barge in narrow waters, gybe her heartily, and without undue refinements. And when you have to run free in the narrows in a strong wind, then—give heed to my example, and reef accordin'.

Her Smiling Virtues

"IS SHE ON?"

Dismay and anxiety are tense in the question. She probably is on; and, if the tide is falling, she is going to stay there. It will be a matter of watching the clock round before she escapes.

And that is where it is that the barge can show herself the virtuous lady. She has none of this crude decisiveness about her. Adept at the mud-game, she will go nosing farther inshore than her deep-keeled sisters; and, even if she overdoes it, and the mud, lying in wait, reaches out a grimy paw and thinks it has got her, even then she will snigger gleefully and cheat him. In sympathetic hands, she will show herself a very knowing and competent little person indeed.

The one thing in chief that she will not forgive is the neglect or mishandling of her lee-boards. Not that any skilful handling is required, for it is simple as A B C. But, first, if a stranger to a barge, you must not forget all about them, which it is quite easy to do; I remember a very good case in point, in running up the Thames. The wind being dead aft, we had gone tearing past Southend and the Chapman with both lee-boards up. But at Lower Hope Point, where you turn up towards Gravesend, course has to be changed. I recall as if it were yesterday how the West Blyth Buoy seemed to come charging towards the yacht on her beam. Down went the lee-board in a hurry; for just in time I had twigged what was amiss.

It is equally easy to forget the lee-boards when getting under way. You get your sails bent and set, going through all the familiar routine. Then you throw your mooring buoy overboard. But, if the lee-board is still up, the yacht is all over the place at once. Until the lee-board has become part of the routine, it is ridiculously easy to make the mistake, because the position of the lee-boards, obvious enough outside the yacht, does not hit you in the eye when you are on deck or in the well.

But, once away, the barge is a treasure in a shoal-beset fairway on a falling tide. My first appreciation of it was just below Pin Mill on the Orwell.

" Is she *on*?" I shouted.

My shipmate of the day, an old hand at barges, merely smiled and 'showed me how' at once. It was, of course, the lee-board, and not the yacht, that had touched. He turned her bows round with the dinghy, and lifted the lee-board as she filled away on her new tack. That was that.

But you mustn't, on your life, lift that lee-board before the appropriate moment. If, before you have the yacht so placed and her sails so drawing as to pull her off the mud, you raise that lee-board 'just to see if it's the board that's holding her,' then you *will* see, and will rue it. She will be hard aground before you can say Jack Robinson. And, if the tide is falling, there she will sit while the clock goes round. Yet, even then, and little as one deserves it, she will still show what Christian qualities she has; for, instead of listing over forlornly at a steep angle, she will sit with her mast as upright as a church spire; and we can at least spend our time of durance on board in complete comfort.

Perhaps I have never realised quite so fully what her possibilities are as one moonlit night in Poole Harbour. *Growler* that evening had just come along from

Swanage, where the south-westerly wind had made the anchorage rather 'roily.' The bay gives excellent shelter from the wind, but the swell comes in, and the yacht behaves accordingly. I have heard one man—and a hardy one—say it has cost him his breakfast. As, therefore, my shipmate and I do not like being deprived of our breakfast, either before or after consuming it; and as, above all, we abominate the racket and disquiet of an uneasy berth, we slipped round into Poole Harbour.

The evening had brought a clear sky, full of wind. Night had fallen, and the moon was up before the yacht reached in, past Sandbanks; and she was going magnificently. A berth off Brownsea Island, at the seaward end, would have been perfectly snug; but the sailing was a delight; and, the tide being high, we decided to go on up towards Shipstal Point, by way of the Wych Channel.

Now on the charts and plans of Poole Harbour there was a great profusion of booms, stakes, withies, buoys, and other objects for the guidance of the mud-mariner. There are rubber buoys now. By day, the marks were much more modest than the chart might lead one to expect—if you except the Main Channel and the Diver Lake (which looked like a hop-field). At night, even under the moon, the marks of the Wych Channel had gone altogether; you could only see them when you stumbled right upon them.

Yet under such conditions there is no trouble, even for a deep-keeled yacht, in a fairly straight channel, when she is beating. She keeps the lead going, and is safe. But when you have a curly channel which sometimes gives you a very long leg in-deed, and sometimes so short a leg that it really is not a leg at all, then you have to be careful. The water was not rough here in the shelter, but the wind was strong, and *Growler* waltzed to and fro with great zest and speed. Brownsea Island, with its rugged groups of pines, towered above (it is quite steep and impressive at the landward end by night, close up); and the yacht dodged this way and that. Theoretically, it is quite easy to follow the windings of the creek, even in the dark. Practically, when the whole harbour is one great moonlit lake, and you cannot for the life of you make out a single withy, it is not easy. If the breeze is light you have time to scratch your head and think. But when the yacht has finished her board almost before she has begun it then things are very much less simple.

If, on that night, *Growler* had been a keeled yacht, she would have finished up her tack (and her night's sailing) by bringing up on the mud at a very early stage.

The tide was on the turn. *Growler* certainly finished some of her shorter boards by locating the mud with great accuracy; but the difference was that she only had to be humoured in the right way and she was off again at once and ready for more. She brought up finally exactly where we wanted to bring her up; and we sat in the moonlight and watched the tide recede. She was anchored, mid-channel, in her own little fairway. I could never have done it without her help.

Yes, in these waters she was a treasure. Here she would confidently perform things that most other yachts of her size might well hesitate even to try.

Without Power

A PROFESSOR OF STRICT LOGIC might contend that, if a yacht is without power, she is powerless. But that is very far from the case. The yacht is a wonder; she gets from port to port in her own inimitable fashion, and she wriggles up the most tortuous of fairways. And then look at her on a breezy day!

To us who sail yachts, the yacht is always a personality with life of her own. She is a creature of the sun and wind, just as we ourselves are. We get our own life from the elements; without the light and air we should perish out of hand. We borrow; and so does the yacht. And she, too, can claim a life of her own.

Not only when the breeze is really ruffling the water is she awake. The faintest stir in the air will set her going. The amount of momentum that a yacht can carry in a seeming calm has sometimes surprised me. Stealing up to a mooring in a wind so light that the water is unstirred and there is no real ripple at her forefoot, how she carries way! And I remember one night, in an East Coast estuary, when I was adrift in a little 15ft boat with sails furled and busy at some small job while the tide was carrying me towards my mooring, a big fishing smack loomed up out of the windless darkness right on top of me. My lookout had been nil, and her side-lights were at the same figure. "Have you an anchor down?" It was a perturbed voice that shouted from the gloom, for the skipper had first spied me right under his bowsprit. Happily for me I had not; and I seized the bobstay and warded my little boat away from her tarry sides. The silent power of the smack's movement in a night that seemed quite windless was a revelation. Both vessels had had the tide

The whole harbour was one great moonlit lake

under them, and this extra momentum of hers was entirely due to some light air that I—at water-level—could not feel at all. I tried for it with a wetted finger, and could feel nothing.

Without power, the yacht is able to do every mortal thing she pleases, provided only that she is not pressed for time. But against the time limit she is bound to rebel, for she knows she will be beaten there. Wind and tide will work wonders for her, but they will do it in their own good time. The sailing man must await their pleasure. I have anchored often enough in sight of my haven, or have stood off and on to await the flowing tide, seeing meanwhile the power boats get home in their own direct fashion long before me. Such a vigil involves a certain philosophy.

But it is not only in the matter of 'getting home' that the yacht without power is found out. By no means; many a time has this been brought home. My ship-mate and I, for example, knew all about it when sailing over from Bosham to Bembridge. Now anyone who stands where Sussex ends (at the mouth to Chichester Harbour), and looks due south-west, will look straight into Bembridge harbour. He can see where the land drops to it in the grey distant island on the horizon. And the wind is generally coming straight from that point—as dead a dead-noser as it can possibly be.

So, sure enough, it was to-day; and thus our tribulation began. The mariner bound from Chichester Harbour to the Isle of Wight ought to leave the harbour against the incoming tide in order to catch the west-going stream outside. But the tide runs strongly into the harbour and takes some mastering. True, there is a slack period between the third and fourth hours of the flood, with seven feet or so on the bar, and the mariner tries to hit that period. But he does not always succeed.

We were among the mariners who didn't. We failed to sail windward down Chichester Harbour from Bosham in the little barge yacht in time to get out on the slack period, and so found ourselves bottled inside until high tide. At last the tide turned, and then the yacht sailed down the harbour and out of it, in the steep, breaking seas that are always knocked up when the wind and tide are at feud. The bar was a mass of white broken water. Those shoal seas on the bar often look very dangerous in a stiff wind. In a really strong wind, of course, the sea closes the harbour to every sort of traffic. But to-day, and at this state of the tide, their bark was worse than their bite.

By this time, the whole ebb-tide was sweeping towards Selsey Bill, and was determined to carry the yacht thither also. With the wind dead foul, the poor thing earned incredibly little on each patient board. It was a regular tussle. We stood as close inshore as we dared at the end of each landward tack, so as to cheat the tide; and the lead was kept going. So we won our way gradually along towards the Winner at the mouth of Langston Harbour; but there the sands stretch farther off shore, and we were driven out again into the full run of the tide. The green seas were coming on board, the spray flew in sheets and the wind shrilled. The clouds that scudded above were low and gloomy, and evening was drawing on. It was just a case for patience and perseverance, and plenty of both. We had to sail ten miles to gain one! Windward work on a lee-going tide is a thing that shows up a barge at her very worst.

We stood as close inshore as we dared

But this crawl alongshore could not last. We had to 'jump off' for the island some time or other—and then! Out in the deep fairway from Spithead, the east-going stream simply seized her and carried her by the beam away and away towards the Nab Tower. How it swept her! She was pointed hopefully towards her objective at first, then at Culver Cliff, and so on. But she was slashing through the water all the time; and, as she began to close the shore down by Culver, she was again out of the strength of the tide. Then, gradually, she made good again; in the late twilight she crept northward once more. The great headland of Culver, piled high in the gloom, was passed. Lights were twinkling ashore, and the Warner Lightship and the Nab Tower were flashing. The wind had taken off with nightfall, and she worked her way warily up the edge of the St. Helens Sands to the Drumhead. As the tide made again, she crept up the narrow channel, guided by the fairway lights, into Bembridge.

With a spot of power to get her over the flood tide at Chichester entrance, she would have made Bembridge with the west-going stream—perhaps some nine hours earlier. But there was a sense of satisfaction when we turned in that night, because, without power, the yacht had made good her little passage in despite of wind and tide; and we used to say that these hazards were half the fun. But now that I am getting older and lazier, well—I have begun to wonder; and the auxiliary engine has since been installed.

On the Way to Cowes

WE HAD A COUPLE OF DAYS UP OUR SLEEVE for reaching Cowes, and we decided to sail to Keyhaven. As we set sail, the rain started; and, though we sailed past Cowes, we never saw the place at all, because the weather was so ineffably foul that the whole Solent was only a blur, and visibility was practically nil.

A rain squall that blots everything from the picture is usual enough; but this particular effort just went on and on. Sailing in this narrow Solent seaway, we might have been in mid-Channel, for nothing was to be seen but wind-whipped waves. True, the coasts took shape over the bows, as a grey blur, at the end of each board; beyond that, nothing.

Personally I can enjoy that sort of thing for a short time, but after a bit it palls. And the smother of rain and spray had certainly palled before we reached the Solent Banks Buoy, and on the shoreward board could just spy the entrance to Newtown River.

"Shall we go in?"

"No," said I, "we won't go in and we won't pull down a second reef. We'll just stick it out as we are."

But I had to eat my own words. The yacht wallowed and strained; the green water washed heavily on board; the bowsprit was lost to sight in every wave as she plunged. The wind howled. There was no escape from the job. Hove-to, we reefed the mainsail, and changed the jib—out of sight of land in the Solent.

In perfect conditions we sailed quietly off the Needles

On the last board—across from Yarmouth to Keyhaven—those steep waves were almost intimidating, so high they reared themselves directly beside us, and so heavily they broke. The yacht plunged, bowsprit under, and a welter of foaming green water sluiced over her decks; then she shook herself gamely free and threw her bowsprit high in the air, only to come down again with a plunge as the bow crashed on the next wave and buried itself. Rain and spray drove over us, solid.

Then, through the grey murk, the outline of Hurst Castle suddenly loomed. In less than a minute the thudding of the waves had ceased as if it never had been. The shinglebank had reached out its long arm and taken us under its shelter. The yacht rounded up into the wind; the anchor splashed and chain rattled after it, and we were busy getting the gaskets on the mainsail.

We cooked our dinner, sitting in the fo'c'sle, while the waves were *wash-wash-washing* just outside, and the yacht was rocking gently. I remember that, putting my hand to my face, I found it thickly powdered all over—it was the dried salt of the spray. Then, after having fed, we ran out the kedge so as to moor her safely against this howling blast (for Keyhaven mud is soft); and I turned out during the night, in pyjamas and oilskins (not a pleasant assortment of clothing), to see that this savage wind had not made her drag. In a night of wind and fury she rocked securely, and I returned to my dreams.

Morning brought one of those contrasts which are the very soul and life of cruising—the brilliant upper-layer of the cameo. Under bright sunlight sea and sky alike were blue and the wind had moderated to a breeze. In these perfect conditions we sailed quietly off Needles-ward, and then put the helm up and sailed over the summer seas on the way to Cowes.

The general assembly of Cowes had for the most part already arrived—a long and scattered procession converging on Cowes Roads, much as the Canterbury pilgrims converged on the Metropolitan See in the days of Chaucer.

Arrived in the roadstead, we found that all seaways lead to Cowes as surely as all roads used to lead to Rome. The fashionable city afloat was gay in the sunlight, and everything was ready for the crowded week that opened on the Monday.

The Old Cowes Week

COWES WEEK IS A FESTIVAL OF SAIL—a survival. Upon Cowes front, I passed within earshot of two Cockney girls. "An' she sez to me…" one of them was declaring, "an' when she sez that, not *taken abest*, not 'arf I wasn't." Those two words 'taken aback' shone like a jewel in a dustbin.

Those words date from the golden age of sail, when sail was an essential part of the world's life. Years ago that golden age has given place to our modern years, but a whole treasury of nautical phrases has survived, and has flowed into the current coin of language.

When a business man says that his plans have "gone by the board," he may not know that the phrase is born of the sea: he may even associate it with a 'board' of directors. And people unversed in sail will freely speak of 'sailing close to the wind' in regard to their own affairs, or of 'hanging in the wind' in speaking of their own hesitations.

As a nation, we once were keenly alive to doings on the blue water in peace time, and not only in war. In the latter days of sail, the holiday-maker at Margate took delight—during his summer holiday—to wear a nautical cap, and to focus his telescope upon the ships that went by. With the passing of sail, the old interest in shipping has declined.

But Cowes still is a centre of sail. True its attraction was at its zenith when the 'big class' was still in being, and more especially when King Edward VII and King George V were racing in *Britannia*. But the 'Cowes Week' still survives.

Cowes is, in general, quiet enough. We have sailed into Cowes on a summer's day in June when there has been little sign of busy life: the blue water has been quiet, and the few anchored vessels asleep. The town also has seemed drowsy, its narrow streets unthronged.

Far otherwise was Cowes when August was upon it. Approached from Calshot or from Ryde, its throng of anchored vessels was amazing. "Cowes, from the distance," as a journalist said, "seems to be fenced off from the outside world by a stockade of tapering masts, as dense as any forest. When you get nearer you are dazzled by the whiteness of it. Everything—with the exception of the one grey battleship, her satellite destroyer, and the black Royal Yacht—is white. There are huge white sails blown out by the fresh wind into curves parabolic, hyperbolic and elliptical, all extraordinarily beautiful."

And at night the lights were legion, fit indeed to bewilder the cruising yachtsman who has left so late his arrival at the berth intended. Ashore, too, in the pleasant dusk and summer night, the narrow streets under their lamplight were packed and teeming. He would be an optimist who, bound afoot from the midtown to the Royal London Clubhouse or the Castle, expected to make good more than one knot over the ground! But there was an air of festival in the place; a spirit of holiday and goodwill was abroad.

But the people in that crowd, as a single glance would show, were not sailing people only. The 'general public' was there, because Cowes Week was a national event.

These happy folk strolled, in the cool twilight and night, down Cowes streets; and, where the lane of houses opens to the roadstead, they paused and lingered. They watched the lighted vessels, and lights reflected in the slate-blue water. But mostly their eyes were focused towards a dark blur which—were it daylight—would be recognised as the escort battleship standing guard

The R.Y.S. Castle faces the Roads

upon the Royal Yacht and the person of the Sovereign. For the King himself was present.

King Edward VII, *Britannia*'s first owner, was a great figure at Cowes. He thoroughly enjoyed the regatta; it was—in his own words—a 'pleasant recreation' save when the abominable behaviour of the Kaiser made it (again in the King's own words) 'a vexation.'

The Kaiser's steam yacht *Hohenzollern* was at that time a familiar vessel in Cowes Roadstead, and the Kaiser was an accustomed visitor. His demeanour to King Edward VII was 'offensive and provocative.' In August 1895, Sir Sidney Lee recorded, in his biography of the King, that the Kaiser's spirit developed darker features than before. "He sought," said Sir Sidney, "to take the control of the Regatta out of the hands of his uncle, the King and Commodore of the Royal Yacht Squadron, and when he was rebuffed for his presumption tried to prejudice the success of the meeting. He at once entered his yacht *Meteor I* against his uncle's cutter in the race for the Queen's Cup, but, dissatisfied with the handicapping, refused to sail, derisively leaving his uncle's *Britannia* to sail the course alone." Although the customary hospitalities were exchanged on board the *Osborne* and the *Hohenzollern*, the Kaiser spoke to and of his uncle in terms of insult. He taunted him to his face… and, in private conversation with his suite, dubbed him 'the old peacock.'

None the less the Kaiser, in his own way, had a real love of yachting. He created Kiel Regatta on the model of Cowes, and he instituted the well-known race from Dover to Heligoland in order to draw the British yachts to Kiel. His own yachts, *Meteor I—IV*, were fine vessels; but *Meteor IV* perhaps never earned a greater reputation—though of a perverted kind—than when she turned berserk, and ran amok. It is a well-remembered occasion, when nearly a gale of wind was blowing. Major B. Heckstall-Smith, who was aboard *Meteor IV*, advocated double-reefing the mainsail (she had no reef-points in the foresail), but the Germans objected:

"Two reefs in the mainsail and whole foresail will too much headsail be; off the wind she runs and will not the helm answer," they explained.

"Then," Major Heckstall-Smith suggested. "Try her without the foresail." But, "Gott im himmels," the very idea shocked them. "She will be all right," said they.

'All right' she certainly was not. Heeled over to an amazing angle, she put her whole lee-side under, and ran off the wind, unmanageable. Worse was to follow: she was pressed down to such an angle that her rudder was half out of the water, and water was pouring into the cabins through some of the skylights. She was utterly out of control, helpless. At one moment, Major Heckstall-Smith thought that she would fill and capsize:

"But," he said, "the captain and skipper and mate or quartermaster stuck to it well and gamely. They never lost their heads, and they did all good seamen could. There were vociferous shouts of 'Grosser Shote!' (meaning mainsheet), but 'Grosser Shote,' or rather the tail end of him, was made fast on the lee bollards, and these were six feet under water! So ease away Herr Grosser Shote we could not.

"'Lug Shote' was worse. If anybody had tried to get at the lug-sheet tackle he would have wanted a diving helmet."[1]

When she was got under control again, the foresail was lowered and stowed; and when she came to anchor, it was found she had seven feet of water in the hold.

---

1   *All Hands on the Mainsheet*, by Major B. Heckstall-Smith.

Meteor IV was not alone in her confusion. The savagery of wind had scattered the race. But three yachts, three splendid yachts of sterner mettle, *Cariad*, *Lamorna* and *Valdora*, had carried on with complete unconcern, and Lord Dunraven in *Cariad* won the King's Cup for 1912.

The annals of Cowes are almost endless, for there the greatest yachts of their time have competed during a hundred and fifty years. Cowes as a town has also been of some importance. In 1808, it was thus mentioned:

> "The Town enjoys a good Trade for the Sale of Provisions, especially in time of War, when large Fleets of Merchant Ships often ride here for several Weeks, waiting either for Wind or Convoy."

Cowes Roads provided an important anchorage; the face of the waters hereabout and in Spithead would be crowded with deep-water vessels, noble of outline, a city afloat. A mere detail, in that world of sail, would be the yachts of the new club at Cowes. Ships towering and splendid would form the main picture, and on its fringes the flitting yachts would be insignificant by contrast. Now the fleets of sail have vanished; the wider roadsteads—untenanted by vessels wind-bound—are utterly deserted. But the yachts still gather at Cowes Week, and Cowes Week remains, in that manner, a survival.

By the middle of the nineteenth century, the chief claim of the place to attention lay in its yacht club. Thus, in 1847, we read:

> "The Royal Yacht Club, consisting of about 160 noblemen and gentlemen, established here for many years, celebrate their regatta annually in August, on which occasion more than 200 yachts and other vessels are assembled, forming a spectacle truly splendid."

So the yachts still meet at Cowes. Grey dawn filters slowly, and light is shadowy on the sleeping roadstead; the town, too, is asleep. The crowded yachts lie to their anchors. Dawn broadens, and day is with us.

The yachts' crews are busy, and the decks scrubbed and made resplendent. The longshoremen, too, are looking to their boats at the steps, for it will soon be "put you aboard, Sir?" In well-appointed cabins, there is the same stirring into life; the town, too, is awakening. What of the weather to-day?

The Old Glory of Cowes

THE OLD GLORY OF COWES WAS THE BIG CLASS. It was my privilege, in races of the Big Class, to be a guest, now and again, in *Britannia*, *White Heather*, *Shamrock*, *Shamrock V*, *Westward*, *Astra* and *Cambria*. I realise now how good it was.

And never was an event more popular than was that splendid race in which *Britannia* won her two-hundredth 'First.' *Britannia* had always been a hard weather yacht; and the weather was her own on the day of Cowes Week, 1930, when she won that race; there was a hard westerly wind and a dirty sea under low scudding cloud. Seven yachts were ready to respond to the starting gun—the six others being *White Heather*, *Lulworth*, *Westward*, *Astra*, *Cambria*, and *Candida*. Every yacht was reefed, but over her reefed mains'l *Britannia* sent up a jaunty little rag of jib-headed tops'l. She had not forgotten her old form.

I was a guest on board *White Heather* that day, and I well remember a start that was worthy of the race that followed. There was the gun! Tearing through the water in this fierce wind the yachts were all in a bunch; all heading for the shore, and the innermost ones shouting for water. Lee ho! We were about. *Britannia*'s helm was down, too, her jib cracking like thunder beside us as it flogged and thrashed. Her bowsprit had been almost at our shrouds. Phew! It had been a close business. *Astra*, *Westward*, and *Candida*, astern of us now, were following *Britannia*. The whole fleet was away—down Solent for the Lepe.

Look at *Britannia* as she goes about again! Cataracts of water are emptying themselves down her black topsides; her lee deck must have been one mass of running water. The wind comes in tearing gusts. And look at *Candida* now! Bad luck! Bad luck! Her mains'l, newly bent to-day, is fairly in ribbons—slit clean across. This is the first casualty of the day, and not the last.

The other six yachts are slashing through the foam: it will be a hectic business at the East Lepe buoy where we all have to gybe. Everyone on board is breathlessly busy. The buoy, as we approach it, seems to hurl itself towards our raking deck, and there is a cauldron of mad white water all round the buoy. One yacht on port tack has held on too long, and a protest flag is in the rigging of another.

"Britannia's in the lead!"

The wind is now just abaft the beam: and—on the reach—we relax and stretch our legs. It is Queen's Course to-day. We are flying now towards the Norman's Fort; and at the Warner we shall have to stay round the lightship. "Mainsheet in! Now's y'r time!" We all jump to it. Hand over hand at first the sheet comes in: then a stop is adjusted. "A pull now, all together! One and hold! One and hold! Ah-hi! Ah-hi! That'll do y'r main-sheet. Come up behind. Make fast!"

So we race on. *Westward* is in the lead, having passed *Britannia*. *Astra* is just leading us, and *Cambria* is not far astern.

"Hullo! Look there! *Astra's* out of it—look at her mainsail!" Her mainsail is slit across, as with a knife. *Lulworth* has, earlier on, been in collision, and has hauled down her flag: this, therefore, is the third yacht out of the race. The wind is even more violent than ever, slashing the green sea in violent catspaws. Our lee rail is submerged again, and the lee deck is one long cataract of white water. Past Norris Castle and onward we thrash to windward, past Cowes and on for the Lepe.

Westward and *Britannia* are fighting it out. *White Heather* can do nothing against them in this weather. If our mainsail does carry away we are done for, for the whole week: we haven't a spare available. Sorrowfully, we fall out of the running—the fourth yacht to retire.

"Look at the schooner! She's simply shovelling it over her decks!" *Britannia* and *Westward* certainly are having a gay time—they are fairly burying themselves in the heavy seas down Solent.

The two leaders are soon back again to Cowes, and once more have disappeared to the eastward now, down somewhere by the Warner. *Cambria* is gamely following them, but far astern.

Here come *Britannia* and *Westward*! They are within sight of home. Yes, there are the sails, but which is leading? Impossible to say. They are roaring home: it is a duel, and a magnificent one. It means one long leg now, right up to the line. Which will prove the closer-winded? Which is it? *Westward*! *Britannia*! *Westward*! It seems to be neck and neck. Hundreds of eyes are strained upon this splendid tussle.

"*Britannia*'s in the lead! *Britannia*'s well to weather!" As the two vessels gradually take bolder size and shape, it is clear that *Westward* cannot weather the battleship. *Britannia* seems a certainty now, unless something carries away. With a white swathe of foam under her forefoot, she comes roaring up past us and on to the line. She is home! The race is won, and what a race! A roar of cheering comes down the wind to us from all the Roadstead. The white spurt of smoke and the belated bang have told us she is the winner. Everywhere caps are waved and everyone is shouting. Westward, a splendid second, is over the line also, and we can see the caps of all on board her waved in the air, while they cheer and cheer *Britannia* to the echo. And, over the shouting, the wind still howls.

The day passes to evening and evening to night. But that boisterous twilight must not be the note on which we finish. One would rather recall the quiet twilight of so many and many evenings when the coppery sunset grows dimmer, and the yellow riding lights, glittering all over the Roadstead, are mirrored in the dark blue water. It really looks like a lake of fairyland in those charmed twilights. And so to bed. May the morrow bring the right breeze for the morrow's race!

A Twelve-Metre Race

T HE START OF EVERY YACHT RACE is a real show of knowledge and skill, but the crossing of the line at the end of the race may *in some classes* prove to be a very tame affair. The yacht first home may prove to be a second or third—or indeed even unplaced, while other yachts, hull-down and barely in sight, may turn out to be the winners.

In a 12-metre race there is no ragged quality. When you have sailed your course justly and aright, no adjustments or calculation or anything else can change your place on paper after the event. First home is first; the winner wins.

Brought to a common footing in the matter of measurement and sail area, the 12-metres fight it out in terms of skill and seamanship. Away with them all at the gun, and the devil take the hindmost! It is fine sport.

By invitation, I was sailing in *Iris* in Cowes Week some years ago. The yachts had been ordered east about. Morning was sunny, but the breeze was shy and uncertain; it had not settled as yet, in fact, to any breeze at all. From the east it freshened at last, a light summer breeze; the gun had gone and the crowd of us were away for the S.E. Middle, in close order, turning to windward.

The start counted for much, and the first few boards for more. Our Corinthian helmsman, quiet of voice, seemed detached almost to the point of unconcern. But he was swift enough of decision. This morning was the first day this season which had brought out a full muster of the twelves; the whole fleet was here, and our helmsman put *Iris* across the line in front of them all. *Vanity* crossed the line second, and *Iyruna* fourth. Doughty combatants there were likely to be, and we watched two of them as they came into company at once. They sailed more or less in company for the whole race, and they sailed away from *Iris*.

"Just the weather that *doesn't* suit us—a calm sea and a steady breeze."

Clearly so. *Iris* was a hard-weather boat, and wanted a blow to make her show her best form. She was not at her best to-day, and the general shuffle of the pack which occurred in the early stages of the beat eastward had left her in a lowly place. *Vanity* led.

"*Vanity*'s got a better breeze out there?"

"No, she sheeted her main in hard, and that improved her."

The 12-metres show their skill and seamanship

For that helmsman needed no adventitious aid of private breezes. He was able to prove that the oldest yacht of the fleet, under his hand, could be the most formidable. And once ahead, he was a difficult man to pass. As we all beat towards the glitter of sunshine on the dancing water, he worked out a gradual lead, and was first round the buoy.

Iris had suffered total eclipse. First away, she was now woefully near the tail, when—after beating in a bunch—the race strung itself out for the run to the Calshot Float. She had, all the same, escaped the very hindmost place and would not be seized of the devil. In point of fact, I noticed—before the race was over—the very hindmost quietly forsook the race and stole secretly home.

Spinnaker to starboard, we were running free. Automatically, I went along to the stern, but I was recalled. "All up in the middle of her," was the helmsman's decision. "She's got a long stern," he added to me.

"Watch your spinnaker—for'ard a little more," was the helmsman's next word, and we were sailing blindfold now, a hand lying on deck to peer under the spinnaker as our look-out man. Jimmy Blair, the skipper, was beside him, trying to see round the corner of it. Then, again, we paid the mainsheet still farther off until we were almost sailing by the lee, and so shaped course for Calshot Float. "Down stays'l now. Balloon stays'l."

The wind was not really settled; it was fitful, and curiously patchy. The thing was interesting to watch. Two yachts beside us were in close company, very close company. But one missed *entirely* a puff which her neighbour got. The one looked just as if she must have a kedge from her stern as the other sailed clean by her and left her standing.

"Get rid of the spinnaker now and ease away the runner." We had to gybe, and over went the sail. "Square her up for the buoy; the tide's running into Southampton Water."

Once past the Float we scattered, some passing the Light Vessel on one side, some on the other.

"The wind's going to play some funny tricks before the day's out," said someone, and we rubbed our hands as we watched the game it was playing at the moment. *Modesty* and *Rhona*, ahead until now, seemed suddenly to stop, and we slid clean away from them, passing them once and for all. We had left two yachts astern already, and this accounted for two more of them.

So far so good, but there were many more to be passed before we could get a place. Should we set a spinnaker? No. Six of the others did so, but we refrained. "She's stopping herself with that spinnaker," said our helmsman, nodding his head meditatively at *Moyana*. So it seemed, indeed. All of them, in fact, handed their spinnakers, but not before we had left *Moyana* astern. Another one ticked off! Come now, this was better; we were well away from the hindmost now. We were creeping up the ladder.

We were soon approaching the East Lepe. Fitted with a double stay, *Iris* could set her next headsail before handing the previous one. In came the mainsheet at the buoy, and we were close-hauled.

For the first time to-day, we really began to sail. In a stiffening breeze we had to turn to windward. When the boards were short, I need not always trouble to shift to the weather side, and a fine sensation it was as one hung on the lee side, one's feet nearly in the water. The waves were thrown, thrown, thrown in foam from that lifting bow; and the white water raced by. This was a change after the languor of the pale-blue Solent of the early morning. The seascape was wind-blown now, vigorous and alive. In the easterly breeze, the edges were cut with a knife.

Here was Cowes again. The tide was running strongly past the Royal Yacht, and we stood close inshore. Then, dodging in and out among the anchored steam yachts, we played hide and seek with our rivals for a time, only finding one another again after Cowes Roadstead was astern, and we were away again for the S.E. Middle. Five yachts were ahead of us, and we should want more wind than this if we were to come up with them in the second round.

"Shall we do it now, Jimmy? All right? Lee-ho!" So we made our last board in the Middle buoy, and the spinnaker was set to starboard.

"Let the spinnaker run for'ard a bit. Get the mainsheet in."

With the spinnaker in this position, we were again stone-blind. The race ahead of us and the buoy for which we were steering had gone. "Where's the buoy? Don't hit it!"

"Tide's taking us to loo'ard of it!" We shortened the mainsheet, easily, not too fast, and past the Float she slid with only a yard or two to spare.

So we were away for the East Lepe again, and it was now afternoon, so that now the sunward glitter was to westward. And again we sailed towards the jumping points of light on the water.

Five yachts were still ahead as we reached away westward, and the wind had steadied again. The leaders had gone from us beyond recovery in a wind like this, but there were still hopes of improving our place. As we approached the buoy, we could see that *Iyruna*, *Noresca* and *Doris* were getting involved in a luffing match, while *Vanity*, clear of them, was opening out. If we were only a little closer up, we might make profit out of it. But... "We'll see what we can do when we're round the buoy and on the wind!"

Clymene, the next ahead, was making a long board inshore. We crossed her track as we turned to windward also, on long boards. Board for board with her we sailed, until we were clearly ahead of her, and she was yet another ticked off, and left astern.

If the race had run to a third round, we might perhaps have continued our process of gradual slaughter, and crept up towards the first place. But our chances were finished. For here was Cowes, and there was *Vanity*—all but over the line. To and fro we sailed in the light easterly wind. This race was done. *Vanity* had got her gun, and we cheered her as she sailed away to her anchorage. Sir William Burton, in *Iyruna*, was home soon after, and the second gun was his. Then came *Noresca* and *Doris*, and after them *Iris* was also over the line and slipping through the crowded shipping of the roadstead.

We furled the mainsail, and Jimmy Blair found that many hands made light work. "Ma crew's gettin' on," he said, with that pleasant twinkle of his. The anchor was down, and we were at rest. The *wash, wash* of the water had been exchanged for silence; movement for stability.

"Peace, perfect peace," said someone.

"Peace all day," said our helmsman, with genial contempt of the weather, "no work for anybody."

One Moonlit Night

A CYNIC IT WAS WHO SAID that there is no joy in cruising and that the only joys are planning out a cruise beforehand and thinking about it afterwards. I don't think he really means it; and certainly I don't believe a word of it. The cruise may have its troubles; but the happy interludes are manifold and wonderful.

The wind had failed us entirely in the western Solent, and the west-going stream was in full control. The tide had just turned and would soon be running like a mill stream, as it always does. So far so good, for we were bound westward ourselves. We wanted to make the North Channel, but really the Needles would do equally well. The one thing to avoid was getting between the two. The Admiralty Pilot Book tells us that the ebb splits about a third of the way between Hurst Point and Cliff End Fort, one part running through the North Channel and the other "setting obliquely across the Needles Channel and over the Shingles with considerable velocity." Later on the directions say that "a strong eddy which runs between the junction of the tides and the Point must be carefully avoided, for, in it, a sailing vessel becomes totally unmanageable."

It so happened that the late and deceased wind had been westerly, and we had been beating. When the breeze suddenly decamped we were beautifully placed to be swept into that blessed 'strong eddy that must be carefully avoided.' If we had jockeyed skilfully for position for it, we could hardly have done better. And, presumably, after the eddy had done with us, it would send us 'obliquely across the Shingles,' with night coming on and a swell running, after the recent wind. "Caution" (the book of the words said) "is requisite in approaching this shoal on either side, for the rapidity of the tidal streams and the violence with which the sea curls and breaks with the least swell over the numerous shallow heads entails almost certain destruction to any vessel driven on it."

We knew all this by heart. For that reason I was in the dinghy, with a tow-rope to the yacht, and trying for all I was worth to tow towards the northern shore. Anchor, you say? Not likely, and miss our tide and our night passage. But I sweated my very soul out at those wretched oars, full of worry, until at last I felt we were fairly in the north stream, and then…

Three cheers, three hundred cheers, there was wind. I had spied it on the water and was ready before it came. Avast all this worry, avast all this sweat. It didn't matter a straw from what direction the wind came; it was wind, and the yacht would be under control once more. The wind—when it came—was a fair wind! We eased away our sheets, and a brisk draught sent the yacht through the North Channel like a train, the full strength of the ebb tide being under her. The Hurst Castle shinglebank was so close aboard that one could toss the proverbial biscuit on to it; past the shore she hurtled and we were soon clear of the narrows and could laugh at eddy and shoal alike.

"This wind, having breezed up after sunset," I had said with my wisest air, "will probably blow all night." The event proved me to be quite wrong, but that didn't matter in the least. We bowled along, lifting and falling to the waves and setting a course for Anvil Point.

Hengistbury Head, on the starboard side, grew into size and shape; but long before we had brought it abeam the headland had become nothing

The yacht was ghosting now

but a blurred outline in the gathering darkness. A perfect night. Behind the headland is Christchurch Harbour, but there was, of course, no sign or glimpse thereof.

Then astern of us came up the great face of the full moon. The wind was now lighter, but we still reeled the knots off quite merrily and sat in perfect contentment watching the magic of the moon-track on the water astern, the twinkling shore lights abeam, and hearing the everlasting music of the water as we clove our resolute way westward. The surface was wind-ruffled and the waves made a merry tune.

Gradually and by imperceptible degrees the wind grew lighter, but still we stole on with that steady gliding movement, on and on. We spoke little; it was a sort of dream, with the movement and the glitter and the quiet tune of the water.

The waves were now vast swellings with smooth surfaces as they ridged under us and rolled away shoreward. When the yacht came down on the farther side of each there was a slight splashing sound; but apart from that, the silence was complete.

Hengistbury Head had faded in the haze and the wind had now gone. Mist. Yes, sure enough, the mist had obscured the horizon and was closing about us. Gybe-oh! We would stand well into the bay and out of the track of shipping. Still the yacht stole on, ghosting now, a shadowy yacht in a shadowy world of mist. The only object visible in sea or sky was the great face of the moon.

"It will be best to anchor before the tide turns," I suggested at last. "This wind won't carry us over any contrary tide." This wind indeed! What wind was there? It had almost evaporated already. But *had* it quite, all? I threw overboard a piece of wood and turned the torch on it. We left it astern quite fast. It is surprising how a yacht can be slipping through the water at a couple of knots without the least sensation of movement.

A glance at the chart had shown me that it would be better to anchor—if at all—east of Boscombe, so as to avoid the possibility of foul ground. We had surrendered ourselves utterly for so long to the charm of this soundless gliding that it seemed almost a sin to bestir oneself in any manner of work. I tried a cast or two of the lead and was more or less satisfied. The anchor splashed down. Even after the sails were furled (soaking wet they were with this dripping mist) I still lingered on deck, enjoying the silence and the vastness of it all. The dew dripdropped from the rigging and the moon flooded the mist, and the yacht rocked drowsily, like a baby's cradle might be rocked. At last I turned in.

Dawn brought clear horizons, a stiff breeze, and the day's work with all its vigour and activity. We sailed on westward. But that night remains in remembrance as a sort of halo-girt memory of moonlight on the sea.

Inside the Sandbank

IN MORE WAYS THAN ONE, Christchurch Harbour is an odd little place. It is a queer sort of haven to get into, and sometimes queerer still to get out of. A stranger yacht might easily sail along the coastline, close inshore, and discover no hope or prospect of any entrance whatever. But vessels of light draft can enter and leave more or less at will, provided that there are not dangerous breaking seas on the bow. At the same time, there is often a spice of uncertainty, even when the seas are modest. The buoys may have been washed away, the shoals may have shifted; and anyway the entrance is right on the beach, with its fringe of breaking waves—which shouts aloud "'Ware shoal."

Yachts even of deepish draught, if effectively piloted, will enter easily enough in chosen conditions of weather. But if during her sojourn inside the sandbank an onshore gale springs up, then on the morrow the bar and the shoals may be found to have shifted in such a way as to have locked the yacht inside the harbour. She is a complete prisoner, cut off from the sea. Many a moon may wane before Nature comes to her assistance, and sends another gale which (if she is lucky) may unlock the door and let her escape to the coastwise seaways once more.

Anchored in Poole Harbour my shipmate and I decided that we would go and have a look at Christchurch again. The books of the words, so far as we could make out their meaning, were not particularly helpful. We were told that the bar dries and is liable to shift. We were also told that strangers should examine the entrance at low water before entering, or, alternatively, should obtain local help. We were also instructed that a gale may at any time alter the position of the bar and render former directions useless. So that now—having mastered all that—we knew all about it.

We made sail and left Poole Harbour, standing away eastward for the Looe Channel, close past the sea wall and groynes and various mischievous-looking objects that protruded from the sea; for that little channel is very close inshore. It was a relief, even in a barge, to be clear of the banks and to be able to edge comfortably away offshore. Past Bournemouth we sailed; and the cliffs of Hengistbury Head stood up over the blue-green seas as if they were an island; beyond the headland and away to the southward glimmered the pleasant island of Wight.

In Christchurch Harbour

Anxiously we eyed the shore as we brought the headland abeam and passed it by; greedily we searched the long sandy shore-line for some sign betokening an entrance. Of sign or token there was none. A buoy? A beacon? Nothing in the world was visible except shore and sea and sky.

On the chart we had worked out our course as near as we could make it, and we closed the shore gradually, with the lead kept going all the time. The wind was a brisk on-shore breeze, and neither of us was feeling in the least confident. Closing rapidly a shallow lee shore, we were hardly to be blamed for it. There ought to be two buoys, and we couldn't see a sign of either of them. We brought the yacht into the wind and peered and peered again. We had been there more than once before, and we knew more or less how it ought to look, but we couldn't make head or tail of it to-day. Some precious gale seemed to have washed up the sand into a solid barrier; there was no entrance at all.

Yes, by Jove, but there it was! There was a tiny speck dancing on the water—a buoy, beyond question. We laid a straight course towards it, and the waves under us were ridging in long lines as they swept in towards the beach. This was not a rough day, yet none the less—as the yacht reached the breaking waves just by the beach itself—she seemed to drop so deeply into the trough that one half expected to hear her hit with a sounding bump against the bottom. We swept on and were almost ashore on solid Hampshire. This entrance plays just the same disappearing trick as Orford Haven does: you close the shore until you seem at the very point of grounding and shipwreck and disaster; you are right on the beach and still there is no sign of an opening.

Then the miracle happens. Suddenly you find that the line of surf is not really continuous. You breathe. Right alongside, right beside the beach, a smooth channel of water leads away and away. All in a moment that lifting and lurching movement has ceased, and the yacht is in a smooth channel with a sluicing tide carrying her towards cottages and trees grouped round the narrows of Mudeford. Seaward of her now a great whale-backed yellow sandbank has shut off the sea entirely from view. Above the sandbank the heights of the Isle of Wight are still visible, a lovely blur of distant blue.

Up the Run we sailed, parallel with the shore. Mudeford was passed, with its picturesque quay and old shore-side cottages and boats; and the tide being high we managed to creep successfully up the shallow harbour behind the bluff outline of Hengistbury Head, up towards the Town Quay. Close beside the latter we picked up a mooring. The Priory, seen across the reeds that fringe the Harbour, was a picture in the sunlight. The whole thing was wonderfully reminiscent of Broadland.

It is a pleasant place in which to bring up. With the Priory on the one hand, and the bold outline of Hengistbury Head on the other, the setting is extraordinarily picturesque and, of course, it is snug as snug can be.

The night was quiet and so was the yacht, and yet I personally was not feeling altogether serene. It seems a preposterous admission, but it is the fact; and the reason was not far to seek. There was a sound on the still air, a continual distant sound. The noise was of the waves breaking on the shore outside. I felt that I was fidgeting quite without reason or excuse, yet I could not help wondering whether this sound of surf was a ground swell heralding a strong on-shore wind. That, if it came, would lock us in, and put paid to the rest of our little cruise.

The entrance to Christchurch had in recent years worked more and more to the eastward, and expert opinion inclined to the view that this gradual progress would not continue indefinitely. In the case of the River Ore, in Suffolk, the entrance has marched no less than five miles to the southward since the days of Queen Elizabeth. In 1813 there was a proposal to cut a canal through to the sea at the old mouth near Orford, but it never materialised. In the same way there has been a scheme at Christchurch to block up this entrance that is creeping eastward, and to cut a new entrance through the sandbank near Mudeford; but nothing has come of it.

We were stirring early next morning in order to get seaward as soon as the tide served and so to capture as much as possible of the east-going stream. That coming storm, as I had known at the back of my head all the time, was only a figment of imagination; and the morning was fine. We set sail in faith and confidence. Two feet is a modest draught, but we had not proceeded more than a few minutes before we were hard aground. Stupid of us, we said, to have missed the fairway, and off we went in the dinghy to locate the deep water. There was none: we were in the best of it already! The tide was, of course, making, and so delay was not unduly prolonged. Gradually, very gradually it seemed, the tide rose, and we crept seaward. At Mudeford a big net was being drawn right across the fairway from shore to shore, and we had to bide our time a little; but we were soon away. The sea was in friendly mood; and the escape was child's play, knowing, as we now knew, what to look for and where. Hengistbury Head dwindled away astern and we scudded eastward, back through the old Needles Channel once more. On the night following I slept the more comfortably for the knowledge that there was no shifting bar between myself and freedom.

To Sea for Shelter

I**T SEEMED AN ODD THING TO DO**, but we did it. Out of harbour we went to sea for shelter.

In a heavy south-westerly blow, we were anchored in Poole Harbour again. We had come in the day before from the westward in heavy weather. Off Old Harry we had seen a yacht's mainsail ripped in half by a vicious gust of wind (we stood by, but she was clear of the rocks and wanted no help, for she had a trysail). The weather being like that, the inside of Poole Harbour seemed at first sight a most desirable spot.

But where should we anchor? Sandbanks would be uncomfortable; and the drawback of anchoring under the lee of Brownsea Island would be that

We were close-hauled and we had two reefs down

one cannot go ashore save by crossing to Sandbanks, in seas that would be too rough for a small dinghy. So we scudded on. Off Poole town there was a regular seaway with much 'froth and bubble'; the whole estuary was a mass of foam caps. Farther up, off that little pier at Hamworthy, there ought to be a snug anchorage, the wind being across the tide. And there it was that we let go.

Snug? Not a bit of it. There was a sharp jobble of short seas, which kept the yacht busy all the time. The wind was as bad as ever in the morning, and we had had enough of it.

"Come on," I said, "let's get out of this." I was grasping the shrouds as I said it; and, frankly, I needed to hold on to something, for the yacht was bucking and flopping to a ridiculous extent. A larger yacht would probably have lain almost rock-steady; but the seas were just the size to give a 10-tonner the utmost degree of discomfort.

"We'll get out of this," we decided. "Item one, it's something to do; item two, it gets us away from this abominable chop."

"Yes, but where?"

"Outside the harbour," I replied. We began to pull down the two reefs that we had only shaken out the night before, and we busied ourselves with a will, glad of the occupation and the prospect.

"We'll go and see what it's like at Studland," was the word. "If it's snug, we'll stay there; if not, no harm done. We'll come back to the 'comfort of harbour' again."

We made a quick passage of it. Off Poole there was an anchored lighter, full of great blocks of stone for the training wall at the harbour mouth. The waves in the fairway were breaking so smartly that the spray went right over her once or twice.

To Salterns we flew. Then we hauled our wind and beat down to North Haven Point, and thence we reached through the harbour entrance in smooth water, going like a train.

As soon as we opened Studland Bay we found the sea rough, despite the shelter of the land; and when we were close-hauled at Punch and Judy, we fairly took it over green. The yacht lay down to work, and thrashed doggedly on. A crash of crockery in the cabin told of minor disaster below; all the ordinary china was, of course, secure, but an ornamental bowl had been imperfectly stowed. Its fragments had a sea burial at Studland.

"I wouldn't have believed there'd be so much sea," my shipmate shouted, as he tried to button his oilskin collar more firmly round his neck. The spray fairly came in sheets. "Why, we're right under the lee of the land, and yet..." Another sheet of spray made an appropriate ending to his sentence.

Then, as we actually closed the shore, the magical change happened. The wind blew furiously still, but it blew on smooth water. We could see the streaks made across it, like the streaks made by gusts across a little inland pond. Close to the pilot cutter, we let go our anchor. We were completely at rest, and comfortable at last.

We walked ashore in the afternoon, over the Downs. And we had a peaceful night, although the wind was as strong as ever. It is an odd fact that the very strength of the wind seems to keep the swell out of the bay; and when the wind moderates the berth often becomes less snug. Of course, we had to be on the *qui vive* all the time. If there were any indications that the wind was backing south-easterly, we should have to cut and run, day or night, before the sea had time to get up and make the bay dangerous. But there was no backing, we were at peace. We had gone to sea to look for shelter—and had found it.

Off St. Albans Head

B Y THE TWILIGHT OF DAWN in Poole Harbour we had turned out of the cabin and looked at the sky. It certainly seemed promising. The Harbour was very peaceful at this early hour: the riding lights of the yachts were reflected in serpentine patterns on the quiet blue water, and the distant Purbeck Hills were dim in a soft purple. We went below at our leisure, and cooked our breakfast.

The sun was up long before we sailed down to the North Haven Point, past Sandbanks, and out to the sea. The yacht stole down the Swash Channel and the sea was blue. On the port side, far away on the horizon, was the distant Isle of Wight; on the starboard side was the chalk cliff and the Old Harry rocks bathed in sunlight. Both sea and cliffs seemed to be deserted: no sign of life was here save the circling seagulls and their distant cry.

As we stood out to sea, we opened the bold faces of white chalk that drop perpendicular to the sea at Ballard Head, and the whole curve of Swanage Bay stretched away southward. We kept our course seaward, and did not hug the shore. We wanted to clear the Peveril Ledge, off which is a race which inclines to be vicious. Having once tried it, we always decided to give it a miss; as soon as we had brought the Anvil Lighthouse abeam, we could steer for St. Albans Head. St. Albans has a race of its own also, and all races are rather disconcerting; but on a day like this it would not be really formidable. We sailed on, past Durlstone Head and Anvil Point, rugged rock-headlands.

"Change course now?"

Yes, we would; we changed course, and were soon sailing due west. It was a crisp sort of day now, and coastline was clear-cut; the sea was blue-green, and there was a fringe of white sunlit foam all along the foot of the gnarled and rough-hewn rocks. This was a splendid day; there was a crisp wind, sometimes hardening to stiff, but never too much. All the sea was bright and full of sparkle. Over these seas, which were swinging landward in ridges, the yacht slid comfortably with an even lift and dip. The great mass of St. Albans Head was no longer distant now; it stood boldly, with every block and promontory modelled in the strong sunshine, and every hollow and gulley black in shadow. And there, seaward to a mile and a half, was the white and broken sea which is the St. Albans race.

The waves hit the boughs and broke on board

There is always a curious sensation as one approaches the race. Sometimes the yacht may be sailing sedately on a foamless sea, and then suddenly she is among white combers rearing up and curling and breaking just as if they were breaking on the beach. Ahead was that waste of green sea, tossing and thrashing itself into white foam.

Perhaps we were sailing too fast as we entered the race. Riding clear over the top of the first wave the yacht drove into the second, putting her jib right into it, and the wave hit the bows and broke on board. The green water and its bubbling foam was swirling aft as the yacht rose to the next wave, and was draining out through the scuppers. The impact had knocked all the speed out of her, and she now took the seas much more easily. Kept head to sea she breasted the seas steadily and, helped by the tide, she forged ahead all the while. On the craggy sides of the headland we could pick out shore marks, and we watched them to judge progress; yes, she was getting on well.

Then gradually the seas moderated, and we were through. Just as before, the yacht sailed comfortably again, and beyond the rocky Kimmeridge Ledges—

upon which the wreck of a steamer was perched—the chalk faces of the cliffs to the west were white over a blue sea. The wind was now taking off a little.

Bound for Weymouth we did not hug the shore, but the grand panorama of those chalk cliffs, white and steep, was splendid all the same. Yonder was Lulworth Cove, and we could locate the entrance by the land marks, especially the Coastguard Station, conspicuous to the west of the point of entry. And so, as the day passed its noon we sailed on past Bats Head and White Nose, basking in the sunshine. Beyond Osmington is the Redcliff Point, and the cliffs dwindle towards Weymouth; on we sailed into a pleasant breeze, while the sparkle on the sea still glittered away to the southward.

Gale Warning

THINGS ARE SIMPLER NOW, since the advent of wireless, I was saying in an old friend's cabin. Though even wireless itself has its drawbacks. "Take my advice," said a hard-bitten fellow who was also there, who was looking round a well-appointed cabin in which a fine wireless set was a prominent feature, "take my advice, and get a good coal-hammer and smash that thing to little pieces. No one who listens to one of those affairs ever gets anywhere. He's always waiting for better weather." The answer was that one doesn't want to blunder into a gale when a twenty-guinea wireless set can obviate the experience. This the hard-bitten one would deride, saying that the mariner only has to put to sea with well-found gear, and then face up to whatever weather may happen. He may be right, but each to his choice. And forgive some of us if we are more prudent than heroic. And so the matter dropped.

I well remember my first introduction to wireless in a small cruising yacht at sea. I was in my old shipmate's yacht some twenty years ago, and I didn't know that he had the contraption on board. The yacht was butting into a dirty head-sea, bound down-Channel. I was at the helm, my face and oilskins streaming with spray, and my friend was below engaged in various odd jobs in the cabin. The isolation was complete, out there on a wind-furrowed green and white seaway, miles and miles off-shore and not a ship in sight. Suddenly a church hymn, apparently sung by several voices, broke out clear and loud. It startled me quite a bit. That the melody did not come from my shipmate I felt quite sure, neither words nor music. True, he quoted verses *at times*, but they were definitely not of the sort 'appointed to be read in churches,' and he had some little ditties of his own also, which similarly were not for use 'in choirs and places where they sing.' Harmless enough, but not always edifying. What was it, then?

As it happened, however, I had tumbled to the explanation before the owner's grinning countenance emerged from the cabin. "You have to turn on the ten o'clock service," he explained, "in order to be sure of getting the weather report." On the occasion that I am recalling "winds fresh to strong" were predicted, and realised. But a few days later a gale warning kept us in port when we should otherwise have made sail, and that gale was a snorter. More than one well-found vessel was in trouble, whereas we, in lucky possession of a mooring laid for a ship thrice our tonnage, merely rocked, rolled and wallowed, and were able to preen ourselves in absolute security.

Things used to be less easy without wireless; and, although as a beginner I had read that, with an intelligent study of the barometer and an elementary knowledge of the main facts of the weather, no man need ever be caught out unaware, my shipmate and I don't think that we can honestly agree.

At times the job requires more intelligence than some of us can lay claim to. The thing may be easy enough when the gale comes up dutifully from the southwest, and is heralded by a barometer that falls like a stone. But when the disturbance comes dishonestly from the north-east, what then? The glass tends to rise for a northering wind, and the dropping thermometer tells the same story— merely that the wind is likely to be from the northward. And then a gale from the north-east comes whooping across the North Sea, with hardly any warning at all. If a signal station were within view of the place where the yacht was moored one would see the gale-warning cone hoisted, point upward; or if one carried a storm-glass it might have clouded. As it was, one sometimes blundered out into quite unwanted trouble, and didn't enjoy it at all at the time, though one tended to talk about it afterwards with some relish.

But there was no fun when our mainsail was torn in two, from leach to luff in a moderate gale from the north-east, when the barometer was over 30. A great tongue of loose sail was slatting and cracking in the gale, and was no use when we were likely to be driven on to a lee shore before we could get the yacht jury-rigged. No, we could not read wisely enough that barometer of ours; prevention is better than cure.

The Eavesdropper

AN EAVESDROPPER IS RECKONED among the meanest of mankind. There is nothing splendid about his iniquity. An eavesdropper is a base person. I am an eavesdropper.

But how can I help myself? When yachts are moored in the tier at Lowestoft, or moored alongside one another as they regularly are at Yarmouth, I.W. (or at any other place, like Heybridge Basin or Ramsgate Harbour, where they are so moored on occasion), the same thing is occurring every day. Mercifully, one cannot hear a word of the conversation that goes on in the cabin of a neighbour's yacht, but every time the people come out into the well, or on deck, I in my cabin cannot help hearing every blessed word of it. I don't like it at all, but I am a prize eavesdropper.

I have mentioned that I do not hear the conversation in my neighbour's cabin in my own; but it is—oddly enough—equally true that I can hear other sounds with surprising plainness.

The alarm clock that wakens *him* in time for his tide is apt to waken *me*; but more than that. The moment a primus stove is started, I can hear it; and when, the passage having been rough and the evening cold, my neighbour feels he has earned it—I can actually hear the spurt of his siphon.

And my neighbour knows a great deal about *my* movements. On some particularly chill morning I announce to him in pride and virtue that I have bathed before breakfast. "Yes," he answers, "I heard the splash."

I tell him that I came back on board rather late last night. "Yes," he answers, "it was about 12." He is polite, but perhaps really means, "Yes, and you made a fiendish row, too, I couldn't help knowing."

But wait until they are out on deck and I am below. Then I hear it all. They are bound from Yarmouth to Poole, perhaps, and the wind, per usual, is strong S.W.

The top of Ballard Down

"We'll get away at nine."

"Tide doesn't turn till twelve, you silly cuckoo."

"Tide be hanged; what's the engine for? Less sea on the lee-going side. I don't want the half-tide rock business if I can help it. No, we'll plug through the narrows without getting quite drowned."

"Oh, of course. I'd forgotten the old stink-box. Ain't we careful of ourselves—what? Mother doesn't like us getting wet."

It is not only on moored yachts that I fill this despicable character of eavesdropper. Take the case of somebody else's yacht upon which a rather noisy auxiliary engine is running. The odd thing is that, although to those on board the noise of the engine quite drowns the voices, the distant listener can hear the words quite plainly. The sound of engine and voice come separately, and the voice is clear as a bell.

A yacht was coming to her mooring under power, and the skipper was for'ard with the boathook while his wife was at the tiller. The dialogue came across word-perfect.

The skipper was an elderly man, courtly (I knew) in ordinary to a degree, though peppery in dispute. We all know how—to the person at the helm—the freeboard of the yacht completely masks the mooring buoy as soon as the buoy is near at hand.

"Put your helm hard over."

"What's that?"

"Put it over, sharp, or I…"

"*What*?" (and a hand is raised to the listener's ear, for she is deafened by the engine).

The response was in the hearing of all men, little as the speaker knew it. The peppery streak had come uppermost by now.

"*Save me from fools. Do what you're told, woman. Put your helm hard over!*"

The two innocents probably do not know to this day that they amused quite an audience on various yachts close by, and even—I believe—on the hard itself.

Finally, the average yachtsman is never really safe while there are nasty eaves-droppers catching shreds of conversation never meant for their ears. You would think you were safe enough when, without another ship in sight, you were sailing in a bluff seaway off some noble headland. Don't you believe it. With a sterling little breeze, the yacht is reaching well and truly, and the waves are breaking from her with a continual tune, so that you have to raise your voice to make your ship-mate hear. He hears right enough, if you raise your voice; but he is not the only one. On the top of Ballard Down (by Swanage), for example, the prize eavesdrop-per has gone for a walk, his yacht being anchored under the weather shore; and there he is. He hears every word that is spoken.

Odd; but true.

The Old Yarns

THE YARNS OF YACHTSMEN have a quality of their own. They have, for instance, nothing in common with the proverbial 'fish' stories, nor with those tall stories that are alleged to belong to the golf-course. It is probable that both fishermen and golfers are grossly traduced by this reputation of theirs, and

I daresay that there are some yachtsmen who tell tall stories also. But the characteristic yarn of the yachtsman is quite different. It may be as sensational as you please, but it must both *be* true and *ring* true. On the other hand, it may be as trivial as you like, provided only that it wakes a responsive chord. The circumstantial detail is all-important. The tale must, so to speak, 'smell of the lamp.' And no credit is given for madcap adventure involving unnecessary risks, especially if embarked on without proper preparation and foresight. That splendid phrase 'proper and seamanlike care' governs the situation.

Stunt-hunters may cross the Channel in all sorts of unsuitable craft. Let them do so; leave it to them. They generally wait for a flat calm for the passage, and when they have finished they are only stunt-hunters after all. The yachtsman demands a vessel and equipment suitable not only to the occasion, but to all occasions, for he knows that a flat calm in the morning may often mean a hard blow before night. And he also knows that a small yacht, properly found and equipped, may—if caught out in a gale—render a good account of herself even when the packet steamers are kept in harbour on account of the weather, and steel plates on big liners at sea are crumpled by the force of the breaking waves.

Often, indeed—a thing which the landsman can seldom comprehend—the safest place for a small boat is at sea, provided, of course, that sea-room is ample; and her most prudent course is to remain there. The best possible proof of this is the case of a fleet of Breton fishing boats which were caught in a sudden gale. All of those that remained hove-to at sea survived, and practically all that ran for harbour were lost. Facts of this sort form the background of the yarns that are current among yachtsmen; yachting at sea is a sport which demands knowledge, preparation, forethought, and prudence.

The man who has brought off great and adventurous cruises may publish a log written in brief and seamanlike form, and will expect his details of gales and other unpleasant conditions to be verified by reference to the official meteorological records. But try to get him, when in company, to spin a fine yarn about his achievements, and an oyster simply isn't in it with him. He will tell you how he got off course through his own folly, or how he lost something overboard through sheer carelessness; and if any jackass in the company begins to tell him what he ought to have done in the circumstances he will probably accept the correction quite humbly.

Then came the steamer, sucking all the water off the flats

In all this he is true to type. Probably the most usual and the most popular of the casual tales told in cabin and clubhouse are those which exhibit the yachtsman in his less fortunate moments. It is the silly little happenings and humiliating little incidents that are treasured and remembered. The tale teller forgets the perfect passage that he made up-Channel, but the fact that he went aground in his own creek at the end of it, or dragged foul of someone else in an anchorage, sticks in his mind for evermore.

Another thing. When the chatter is in full spate in the clubhouse, it is not the instructive account of unknown regions that holds the audience; unless the raconteur is skilful beyond the ordinary, the little group about him is apt to melt and dwindle. If, on the other hand, he speaks of some grubby little shoal round the corner, into which we all blunder at times, then eyes sparkle and the small knot concentrates and grows. "Don't I know it?" says someone. "There's a tail on the shoal there, and I believe it's shoaling out farther." "It's picked me up, too," says another. The yarn is a success beforehand, and everyone leans forward, breathlessly interested. It is of the places that we know already that we love to hear.

Try asking a man about his holiday cruise. A fellow the other day was asked about a recent cruise of his in which he had encountered some pretty dirty weather. He spun the regulation yarn. He said that he very nearly bungled the entrance to Dover, that he was frightened to death off Beachy Head (no other detail of the passage was vouchsafed), so that he was thankful to get into Newhaven—a harbour which he described in full from the inside and stigmatised in caustic fashion as a "beastly hole."

But what he really warmed to was an incident at Lymington, where practically all the available space is taken up with moorings. Trying to find a berth outside the fairway of the packet steamer, he went in too far and got aground. This mattered little as the tide was rising; so he and his mate retired to the cabin and set out the crockery for a meal while they were waiting. Then came the steamer; it was of the old paddle type, long before the present 'ferries' had appeared. The steamer, owing to its displacement, sucked the water off the flats as it approached. This instantly threw the yacht over at a heavy angle, and sent every bit of crockery with a crash to the floor. He told it well. His whole story was a great success, but he told us not one word about that hard fight to windward against heavy seas.

On another occasion, when several yachts had anchored in a West-Country roadstead, a few of us were together in the cabin of one of them. The conversation turned on navigation, and the company began to get on well towards spherical trigonometry. Then one of us who, silent hitherto, had bent a humorous eye upon the group, intervened. "*That's* not the way to navigate," he said. A chart was on the table and he put his hand upon it. "I came to this place from Cherbourg, and I laid an honest compass course without any refinements, like I always do. I didn't hit *this* place, but I got somewhere else, up there, I suppose," and he airily indicated a bay full of rocks. "Well, we've hit old England, anyway, I said to my mates," he continued, "and that's something, but I hate the look of this corner of it, so yo-ho, my hearties, we'll try somewhere else. That's how we got here," he concluded. "Nothing simpler, and I don't know what all you fellows are talking all that rot for."

Truth to tell, the speaker was himself as finished and learned a navigator as ever sailed a yacht.

Man Overboard

I tell this tale which is strictly true
Just by way of convincing you…

R UDYARD KIPLING, when he wrote those two lines, simply meant that he was just going to work off a particularly tall story. But *these* little yarns are fact; and I need hardly say that they are comedy also. It is easy enough to come upon stories that are quite the reverse, and it is in no light strain that one writes of *them*. But when it's 'all's well that ends well' everyone is pretty sure to laugh. The only fellow who does not taste the joke is the man who did the header. He grins, too, perhaps, and looks sheepish.

Now this fellow asked for it. In a small cruising yacht, running free in Spithead, with the wind dead aft, he went messing about with something down near the runner, stooping over it—his back turned to the mainsail. The yacht was fairly reeling off the knots; and, as she rolled, the boom kept on giving a nasty suspicious lift which makes the helmsman on guard to prevent a gybe. Instinctively he shoves his tiller down a bit, although the lifting of the boom may only be due to the sea. Anyway, he is on edge a bit about it, because following seas are chucking the yacht forward and making her sheer extravagantly. "Come on aft, you silly ass," he shouts; but the silly ass only looks over his shoulder and grins.

Then comes Nemesis. The great boom (for all the world like a mighty rod) swings over and fairly hits him with a proper smack just on the part of the body made for smacking.

If the ditch had not been ready for him he would have been seriously injured by a blow of that force. As it was, the boom shot him clean overboard, just as a boy

The helmsman flung a lifebelt

might bat a ball. The helmsman flung him a lifebelt, and—at the pace the yacht was sailing—he was a pretty considerable distance off before he had rounded up and hauled in his mainsheet and brought the yacht on the wind in order to return.

Needless to say, it ended happily. He was not a penny the worse. He was smoking cigarettes and calling everybody but himself a blamed fool. But he had only got what he asked for, and he might have got a great deal more, as he was told in quite unvarnished English at the time.

And now for another yarn. I was not there, but I had it from a friend who is not accustomed to drawing the long bow, and he assures me that it is literal fact. He and his partner were taking out a couple of fellows who were novices at the game but were intending to buy the yacht. The old hands wanted, of course, to show themselves models of proficiency, and were playing the oracle to their hearts' content. "It's quite simple if you do it like this, but always remember…" and so

139

on. All went well during the sail, and then came a lesson in picking up the moor-ing buoy with neatness and precision. They shot the yacht quite accurately, and the junior partner reached down for the mooring buoy. Why he didn't use a boat hook I don't know. Anyway, he leaned down to grab the buoy and got it; but he leaned a little too far and over he went into the water, hugging his trophy still, and came up spluttering. There were roars of laughter when they got him on board, in which he joined to the full. "Well, little things of that kind *will* happen if you're careless; but, come along now," said the senior partner, "now I'll show you how to furl the mainsail and leave everything snug." He meant to make very smart work of this. The work proceeded and he passed the first gasket, and gave a smart pull on it. But the other end of the gasket was loose, and the whole thing came away in his hand, letting him backwards. The little bulwark behind him caught his heel, and head over heels he went into the water. A spring tide was running, and he tells me that he really had quite a bad few minutes himself because they were all so doubled up with laughter that they could not get the dinghy off to his rescue for quite an appreciable time. In fact, they were all looking a bit grave before they actually picked him up; but 'all's well that ends well,' and the laughter was re-newed over the steaming coffee in the cabin that night. And even now they don't let him forget it.

That same man (and he is reliable) must make a hobby of this sort of thing, for he told me another case of 'man overboard' which might have ended seriously. It was off Orfordness and in a very nasty lop of sea. There were just the two of them on board, and his partner, sea-booted, missed his footing as he got up to do some little job, and went overboard head first while the yacht had full way on her. He had tottered before he lost his balance; and the other man—with that quickness of hand and eye that the yachtsman generally develops— grabbed him (it was a miracle of swiftness) by one of his legs. This meant that the man overboard was towing *head-under*, and would drown. Lightning decision seemed wanted. If he were let go the man's boots would take him down, and he would drown. If he were held there head down the man would drown also. By supreme good fortune the problem solved itself. The yacht, coming into the wind against the head seas, stopped herself completely, and the man on board was then somehow able to grab the other end of the fellow in the ditch, and to get a rope round him. Both were utterly exhausted with their efforts; and it was quite a time before he could even try to get the man out of the water and up on deck. There was no laughter that time. It had been a narrow shave, cut about as fine as anyone could cut it. But, once more, 'all's well that ends well.'

Beyond the Sunset

THERE IS THE VERY SOUL OF OLD ROMANCE in the thought of sailing away into the sunset, just as when Ulysees, "seeking a newer world," said:

> *... my purpose holds —*
> *To sail beyond the sunset, and the baths*
> *Of all the western stars until I die.*

Unfortunately, in our latitudes, there are very many evenings when no sunset is to be seen; and here is a case in point.

We had sailed at speed out of Poole Harbour with one reef down, and had sailed in grand style to Standfast Point and past the Old Harry rocks. Then, clear of the land we faced the grim sou'wester, and a seascape that seemed to have upon its surface almost as much white soap-suds as it had green water. The glass had been rock-steady, and we had expected that the wind would be taking off. It apparently had no such intention.

Whoosh! The spray raked the yacht; it streamed down our oilskins and blinded us momentarily until we could clear our eyes again. Then the next wave did the same. Not very comfortable, but all in the day's work, and we were really working to windward—the shore marks showed that. It was really exhilarating and jolly— while as yet we were fresh and jolly ourselves.

Then came a thud which shook the yacht, as the first big wave—in hitting our bows—sent the green water sluicing over the deck. Well, the scuppers were unclogged and perfectly effective, and the green water could stream back into its element. We stood off shore on a long board. The land would give us little protection, and we intended, anyway, to be clear of the Peveril race, which can be quite nasty. The yacht was buoyant and confident as her bowsprit cut the sky each time

141

she mounted the crest of the waves. But the sting of spray and the sluicing of the green water along the deck had become the day's routine, and the little ship certainly was rather like a half-tide rock.

After three hours' punching into head seas, however, we could not honestly say that Durlstone Head had really been left far astern, and the tide would very soon be turning against us.

We were less chirpy now than we had been off the Old Harry. A few hours of that bombardment of salt water does tend to make one grim rather than songful; but we were in quite good fettle and had an excellent meal, in turns, in the cabin. Before leaving the cabin I had looked at the barometer and noted that it was falling. With a stiff headwind already making things rather lively, that was not a welcome development.

As I emerged from the companion, my shipmate was silhouetted against a dirty sky of driven cloud; and, as I crawled up into the well, the scene astern was an expanse of green-grey seas and grey-white foam, very empty and desolate.

My shipmate was very cheery; his meal had done him a world of good. But he didn't think much of our progress.

"We've made a poor start," he said; "we ought to have come out of Poole against the tide. After the tide turns out here, I doubt whether we shall be able to make any headway at all. If we can work well off shore, and if that rising of the glass means anything at all, we ought to be able to make good headway on the west-going stream. And if the weather goes on being as blustery as this we can of course sneak into Portland."

"The glass is falling," said I.

That made him less buoyant, and an extra vicious deluge of green water came over the bows.

He and I have no heroic bent for 'sticking it out' and we certainly weren't going to spend half the night bucking about like this without any progress. I always remember those words of an old yacht-master, thrashing up-Channel twenty years ago in a three-reef dead noser.

"Come to that," he said, "we can hang on as long as ever we like, only it'll wear all of us out, that's all." And under such conditions, I confess that we prefer a handy port.

And so we decided. Up went the helm, and our whole world was changed in one instant. Instead of that jerk and pitch, that turmoil and endless racket, we had the long lift and fall of the following sea. No 'beyond the sunset' nonsense for us this time; the west was one great smudge of dirty grey cloud over a dirty sea.

Thrown off our course time and again by the powerful surge of those following seas, we swung onward at speed, and the day darkened to desolate twilight. We had soon lost sight of the Anvil lighthouse, but, as the night set in, we located the light of the Poole Bar buoy. The buoy was lifting and wallowing in quite a brisk fashion as, with this quartering wind, we went by it at speed and racked up the Swash. Before long, we heard the *clang-clang* of the bell buoy and we shaped course for the Wych Channel, where we let go under the lee of the solid land of Brownsea Island.

We were neither ashamed nor disappointed. We felt we had done the prudent thing, and the meal which we enjoyed quite ravenously in this haven of peace had a real zest, comparing our snug berth with that riotous sea outside. The glass continued to fall, and that made us even more self-satisfied.

Two days after we glided down the South Deep, and gybed at the buoy off North Haven Point. And thence we had a fair wind all the way down the Swash Channel—a wind that was dead aft. Indeed, we weren't sure whether the boom would not at any moment tell us that the yacht knew better than we did where the wind really was. There was an ominous flutter in the sail once or twice, but each time the helm went down and the sail thought better of it. After that we did what I believe is regarded by some as very heretical; we lashed the boom to the lee shrouds, and were no longer in fear of a sudden gybe. We estimated that the wind was a little north of north-west just then, though later on it was a little to west of it. But nothing mattered; everything was fair and bright, and we were as happy as schoolboys.

Off the Old Harry rocks we hauled in the mainsheet and sailed briskly with a sterling beam-wind. The sea sparkled in the sunshine, and was much less 'lumpy' than one might have expected after a couple of days of really strong wind. This is always a puzzle to me. After a hard blow the sea sometimes seems to calm down in a miraculous fashion almost at once, while on other occasions it seems to keep up its vigour long after the wind has died away altogether and the wretched

It was a joy to feel the yacht slipping through the water — westward

yacht is left to wallow, with her boom flogging and cracking this way and that. No doubt these vagaries are governed to a great extent by the conditions which obtain down-Channel and out in the Atlantic; but several times, after looking at the meteorological charts after the event, I have still been left guessing.

When we had opened the Anvil lighthouse, we began really to make good sea-miles to westward and seaward; with the sheets well home, the yacht was close-hauled to the wind and was sailing well. There was more life in the sea here, and the yacht threw the sunlit foam about quite a little. This was perfect sailing, and our mood changed with it. No longer the *dolce far niente* now; we were mariners once more, and sailing under perfect sailing conditions.

Close-hauled to that splendid north-westerly breeze we now stood away seaward, clear of the St. Albans race and opening, far and far away, the long cliff-line that leads on to Weymouth Roads. It was only a dwindling line on the horizon as we sailed on seaward, close-hauled, with sails bellied into gracious curves, and a white wake streaming and bubbling astern in this golden sunshine.

We made a board or two shoreward, and took care to locate the Shambles Light Vessel as soon as possible; then, when the L.V. became a prominent feature of the seascape, we stood resolutely seaward on a long board, until we had brought Portland Island to the north of us. After that, a diffident board or two landward kept us on our westward way, and we were ready all the time to shy off like a frightened horse at the very first symptom of the fringe of the Race. I have been there, and I don't like it.

The brilliant morning had become the golden afternoon, and the afternoon was declining to evening. Would the wind hold, or would it fall light with the sunset, as the wind so often does on days like this? The sunlight on the generous curve of the mainsail was more and more golden, and the sea—though still full of life—was a summer sea. Portland Island was a thing of the past: we were in West Bay.

Then sunset came; there was a rich brown bank of haze, above a sea of a delicate green. Our side-lights had been trimmed and lighted, and were now set in their brackets on the shrouds: the day was over. To the eastward, the distant Portland light was stabbing the dusk; but still the wind held—the glorious wind held.

There was no chill in the twilight. We could comfortably lounge in the well, and it was a joy to feel the yacht slipping through the water with that regular heave and splash—westward.

Above us the stars were now bright, and to westward was the haze of the faded sunset. The water was still luminous, the waves crinkled with the breeze. We could see the long patterns of bubbles strung out astern, and fading into the darkness; the yacht was slipping through the water, on, on, on. My shipmate's pipe glowed in the dark like a big red star as he settled himself still more comfortably in the well.

In that charmed atmosphere I ventured to quote the lines from "Ulysses":

> *... my purpose holds*
> *To sail beyond the sunset ... till I die.*

"Yes, old man," said my shipmate briskly, "but it isn't always like this. It's more often like the day before yesterday," he chuckled, "when we turned tail and ran for shelter; we didn't have much truck with sunsets then!"

Brutal, perhaps; but, I fear, rather true.

That Same Zig-Zag

IN GRIM CONTRAST TO THE QUIET PASSAGE is that long zig-zag, when the wind is foul and strong, and the night is dark.

The night was as black as the nether pit; and, as I stood at the helm, I could see nothing except the greyish blurs on the dark sea which were the crests of foam.

I don't know whether it is any good to duck one's head from the spray. If free of the helm, one can half-turn and lift a shoulder. That *does* tend to cover the vulnerable spot—the collar. But the trickles seem to get in. Sometimes I have thought that I had made a job of it, only to discover, when I 'undid' myself, that the collar of jersey and jacket alike were soaked and soggy. A small towel round one's neck, with the collar firmly buttoned over it, will sometimes save the situation. But there are some occasions when nothing but a diving suit would guarantee dryness; and to-night was one of them.

My shipmate and I were in a yawl butting resolutely across West Bay in that series of long diagonals, to and fro, to and fro, which has almost become the acknowledged way of getting westward across it.

"I bar the rain," my shipmate said. "I don't mind the salt-stuff. This everlasting volley never stops, and it's getting me as limp as a wet linen-collar." "Bed ashore would be the better bargain, eh?"

He evidently thought so. He became mildly profane, while he grasped the coaming of the well with one hand to steady himself against those *jumps* that a yacht gives when a big wave hits her, and with the other hand he held the collar of his oil-skin close to his throat. Then came his jolly laugh. "It's all in the game," he said.

The waves to windward were heavily capped with foam, and the yacht—as she lifted and dropped—was churning the dark water into spume. Despite one

Thank Heaven for daylight!

reef in the mainsail, the angle of the deck was pretty steep, and that grey streak of foaming water, time after time, came creasing along the covering board. It disappeared as the yacht lifted. Then a fresh torrent followed. And the whipping scurry of spray was a real whiplash on one's face—even on a face well pickled and seasoned already.

'All in the game,' as my shipmate had said. And that jolly laugh of his which had accompanied the remark was—I thought—a bit of an achievement. I envy him that laugh. I can at most times grin cheerily enough myself, and can even achieve a sort of cackling noise, but a full-blooded authentic laugh like that is a gift; a pleasing gift on a dirty night in West Bay.

We were on port tack, and therefore headed inshore.

"That's the loom of the land, I expect," my shipmate said, for the rain had suddenly ceased, and there was a sense of horizon in the darkness, which there had not been before.

"It ain't," I snapped back crisply; and he laughed again, a veritable guffaw.

Nothing, of course, was visible; and the land was miles away. But the fact is that one is much happier on such a night at the seaward end of one's board; we should have liked to be in the Bay in order to cheat the contrary tide; but we had no intention of getting embayed on a night like this.

"You know you're in the English Channel," he twitted me, "beyond that you haven't the foggiest notion *where* you are."

Had he spoken five minutes earlier he would have been right enough. Our computations might of course have been put all wrong by some error, multiplied by each board, and very big in the aggregate. But he spoke five minutes too late, for I had spotted a light—or thought I had—and only waited to speak until I was sure.

"Haven't I?" I said, and I pointed where the tiny pin-prick had stabbed the darkness. "If you take a bearing of that light, you'll know something about it. That's the Start."

"Gosh!" he said, "one up to you."

Morning followed. On such a morning you cannot possibly say at what moment you had first perceived the coming of day. It steals in, and day is beginning. The heavy grey of the night sea becomes the dark grey-green of the dawn. Over the grey welter of it, miles away, the landfall looks remote and tiny.

The breeze was taking off; morning was here. It was one of those occasions when we were thankful for the first grey glimpse. As Paul fought with beasts at Ephesus, so we had fought with demons of misgiving through those dark hours that precede the dawn. Thank God for the daylight!

The Threshold of the West

OUR PASSAGE HAD BEEN UNEVENTFUL. The wind had not headed us in the usual resolute fashion; it had given us a friendly slant from the south. But now, towards evening, while still true in direction, it seemed again to be failing in volume. Over a calm seaway we could see a remarkably long coastal panorama just now; from Golden Cap to Berry Head the coastline stretched, making two sides of an angle, so to speak; and there, in the angle itself, right in the very corner, was our objective—for we were bound for Exmouth.

Somewhere over there the opening must be, but it was miles away as yet, for Sidmouth was still on our beam, ten miles distant.

"We won't get in before nightfall at this rate," one of us said, glancing at the time, "and we shan't save our tide up the river." But, even as we spoke, the wind took heart again, and the low red cliffs at Budleigh Salterton began to be less remote, while the high wooded cliffs of the Sidmouth Coast ceased to hang on our beam. Beyond Budleigh Salterton is Straight Point, somewhere off which is the bell buoy that marks the beginning of the Exe Fairway. We were getting on.

The only fly in the ointment was that we had very little tide to spare; and, if we failed to save our tide up the river it meant anchoring outside—for the tide runs hard. The breeze was fairly good now, but was not of that commanding quality that conquers strong tides.

The yacht lay over, and a very respectable little wake of greenish-white water paid tribute to our progress. We were going to make a race for it anyway. "There's the buoy!"

We had both been straining our eyes in the direction in which we expected the dark speck to materialise, and the one who spotted it first had the usual little note of triumph in his voice. It is a funny thing that one can so seldom *locate* a distant buoy by means of field-glasses; but, once located, the field-glasses immediately make it so clear that one wonders how it had been possible to miss so clear an object before. Yes, that was the buoy right enough. A quiet sea is a blessing in that respect—it makes the buoys so much more visible. In a rough seaway, when perhaps it is important to spot a fairway buoy early, the buoy gets mixed up with the dark contours of the waves, and often cannot be espied until after the unfortunate mariner has suffered the torments of the damned, thinking that he has missed the true channel and is driving to wholesale destruction. Then, when he has suffered enough, the buoy bobs up, just where it ought to be, and singularly close at hand. We had no excuse for agonies to-night. To make the fairway entrance was literally 'plain sailing.'

The wind freshened still more, and the yacht was moving in style. The dark red headland was nearer and nearer. There is really nothing at all to fear

The bell buoy marks the beginning of the Exe Fairway

on this side of the fairway buoy; but after the bell buoy the mariner has to beware. There are rocky ledges to northward and sandbanks to southward. The channel is buoyed, but it is less straight than it looks on the chart, and the buoys were small.

"Can you hear the bell?"

Yes, there it was—the *clang, clang, clang-clang, clang* of the bell buoy. We could see the waves breaking on the Pole Sand. Yes, we were making good our passage; we were going to save our tide.

"Not that it matters," we said. "A night at anchor outside would be no hardship on a night like this."

The tide was still running strongly, and we slid rapidly onward. In shelter of the Pole Sand the water had become very smooth; but we could see the waves breaking outside, both along the line of the Pole Sand itself and the Monster Sand beyond. A small yacht was sailing up the inside swatchway, close in to the low sandhills of Warren Point. We were now in the buoyed channel, and, with chart before us, were ticking off the buoys one by one. While still at sea we had hardly seemed to make progress in hours; here in the smooth water of the sheltered channel we seemed to be slipping up at speed.

The evening was golden—a little too golden, in fact, for the low sun was too directly in our eyes. The red cliffs astern, in this evening sunlight, were redder than ever. And on the water, as we scanned our own fairway for the next buoy, were a thousand dancing flecks of sunlight which dazzled our eyes and made us see double and treble.

On the starboard hand the red cliffs gradually fall to nothing, and the promenade of Exmouth leads up to the little town itself, with its square church tower. On the port hand the narrow ribbon of sand-dunes encloses the tidal waters of the Exe estuary. We were level with Warren Point; we were leaving the sea—entering the Exe.

It is possible to anchor off the pier, but this is not recommended, as the tide runs out so very strongly in that constricted little 'gut' through which the whole tidal lake has to empty itself on the ebb. A steamer was at the pier, and behind that (knowing where to look) we could see the masts of yachts and other vessels in the dock. If one wants to be handy to the town the dock is really the best place. On the present occasion, however, we were well provisioned, and were well content with an anchorage farther off. It was necessary to close-haul the yacht in order to make the next reach, as there is a sharp elbow-bend. Then, beyond the Bullhill Bank, we let go. The sun was almost down, and we lay in a great landlocked lake.

Inclined though we were to be sleepy after the passage, we set forth in the dinghy after sunset. We would not be denied the pleasure of sensing the quality of this secluded corner of our own. The great lake was streaked and rippled by the wind. We pulled across to the sandy shore and looked out over the dunes to the flat sand beyond and the sea that was now grey in the twilight. Another little passage made good.

A Riddle Solved

THERE IS NOTHING SO PREPOSTEROUSLY SIMPLE as a riddle—once the answer is known. The answer is so obvious that any fool ought to have been able to think of that. It fits the case like a glove. Yet no one seems able to hit on that answer; the stock reply is: "Give it up."

Many years ago we had approached Dartmouth with an onshore wind. We had never entered before. Locked in somewhere behind those foam-beaten cliffs was a desirable harbour—but where? From the coast itself, when one is close inshore, everything is so easily identifiable; the headlands jut out like headlands ought to, and the detached rocks (such as the Newstone) are really detached. But, from the offing, they are all flattened together into a single great wall; and with an onshore wind one dare not close the shore overmuch for closer inspection. There are nasty little outliers, the Cod Rocks, the Nimble, the Boatfield, and others.

"Where is that plaguey little lighthouse at Kingswear, or any other blessed thing? Blest if I know, and we dare not go closer in. After all, I think we'll have to funk it and to make Brixham or Torquay instead.

" If this darned wind hadn't shifted and breezed up so hard, we could have picked our way in, cautiously and in comfort."

The wind was not really hard, it was only a healthy full-sail breeze; but circumstances alter cases; and at the moment that easterly breeze was an abomination.

To anyone 'locally acquainted,' the whole thing is so grotesquely easy, and the fair wind is an amenity instead of a plague. Just in the same way, with a pilot on board, a stranger might well wonder that anybody would think of steering a course other than the true one; the problem discloses its own answer stage by stage—and there you are.

In the meantime we pitched and rolled with an easy movement on a genial and sunlit sea. I spotted them, all in a moment, the Kingswear Castle and Dartmouth Castle—yes, there they were.

"I've got the answer to my blessed riddle," I said; "I believe I can see at last where we are."

It was not very long before we were anchored in an inland lake which looked as if it had nothing to do with the sea at all. Lofty slopes surrounded it, and houses were on the hillsides and right down to the shore. Visible sign of the sea there was none. It might be miles off.

There was something a little Continental, we thought, about the appearance of Dartmouth; but Greenway and Dittisham were pure English. When later we glided up with the tide (past that curious Anchor Stone planted so inconveniently almost in mid-channel), and anchored beside the wooded slopes of Greenway,

The open sea is beyond

the picture on every hand was real English and as near perfection as anyone could wish. The picture has since been rather disfigured by modern houses.

Bound seaward once more, we found that the 'riddle' solved itself with a completeness even more striking than before. What could be simpler? Bend after bend of the river discloses a new reach, and then Dartmouth Castle appears, jutting out at the last bend, and the open sea is beyond. But looking back a mile out at sea, the great walls had closed again.

Later on, we knew our Dartmouth well, and sometimes we anchored seaward of the Castle, outside the entrance. It is an old pilots' anchorage, and the holding ground is good. Up to the foot of those craggy cliffs you sail, and then round up into the wind. You could almost chuck a biscuit ashore.

When you anchor in this berth the noise of the waves breaking on the rocks right beside you is heard all the time—the break and scatter of spray and the cascading recoil. It is a sound that I don't really like right under the stern of an anchored yacht. A pilot would not trouble two pins. Knowing that his ground tackle was sound and that the holding ground was good also, he would be perfectly happy. For our own part, we have kept the mainsail loosely furled and the staysail loose enough also for instant action if we saw the slightest sign of the anchor dragging. The wind came in gusts, and the yacht snubbed quite sharply at her cable; then she described a little curve and recovered, and then snubbed hard again. We only anchored there because we could not make our harbour and we slept with one eye open. The auxiliary engine has changed all that.

In Hope of Haven

IT IS A SINGULAR THING THAT, the moment one has decided that a night in harbour is a thing to be desired, the idea becomes fixed and absolute. Westbound, we had rounded Berry Head and Start Point. We had left the shelter of Start Bay, and had hauled our wind. The wind, though not so hard as to justify a reef, was quite hard enough to give us all we wanted. Skies were grey, and the seas broke into little caps of white foam. Each crested wave would hit the bows of the yacht, and the spray scattered. But these waves were regular and large. There was none of that vicious hammer-blow which shorter waves deliver when they break full on the bow—a blow which shakes the yacht all through and kills all her speed. We were sailing well.

Across Lannacombe Bay we beat; and we opened Bolt Head beyond Prawle Point. This was fine sailing, and we ought to have been having the time of our life. But there is always some fly in one's pot of ointment. We were already computing how long the friendly tidal stream had to run, and wondering how far we should have made good. Really it didn't matter two straws if we had a night out, but we wanted a night *in*. And here, off Prawle Point, we were wondering whether our tide would last us out to Cawsand, in Plymouth Harbour; and the answer was No. Salcombe?

On the shoreward board we were able to look into Salcombe, and perhaps we cast a lingering look towards it as we steadied ourselves against the movement of the yacht while she thrashed through the dark green seas. Almost drugged with the strong sea air, we had no wish for a night out. After all, a well-earned meal and a well-earned bunk are the fitting crown for a blameless day afloat, more especially after a turn to windward. It *is* tiring.

"Courage, my hearty," I laughed, "our holiday joys won't last for ever. We shall make longer legs of it after Bolt Head."

"Courage be hanged!" he laughed in reply. "This is perfectly grand, but there's reason in all things. I like a good night and not a rowdy one. What a soundbox the old yacht is when you go below! You can hear every biff the seas give her; you can feel her shake when she's battered; you can hear the water gurgling round her, just as if it were streaming in. I have learned every sound of it, but I don't sleep properly through it."

We anchored seaward of the Castle, outside the entrance

I believe that most fellows, after a trick at the helm, can fall into a perfect torpor of sleep the moment they 'hit the hay'; but my shipmate, in his dislike of a turn to windward unduly prolonged, was orthodox enough. I have heard the toughest of cruising men say that they never turn to windward for more than twelve hours on end if they can help it. They make some haven if opportunity offers, and ensure a good night's rest. On serious passage-making, with a full crew, the matter is radically different. But, with a crew of two coast-crawlers, like us, windward work day and night is making hard work of it.

The succession of bold cliff-faces between the Bolt Head and Bolt Tail is a grand piece of coastal panorama, but we saw little of it to-day. The Ham Stone is usually a 'mark on the course,' so to speak; but not on this passage; we seemed to miss it altogether, because one of our boards took us offshore before we reached it, and the next carried us inshore again after we were past it, somewhere in the region of the Bolt Tail. I remember noticing how the waves were spraying up over the rocks at the foot of the Bolt Tail; but I can recall little else of the landfalls during this latter part of the passage. What I remember is a salty deluge of spray and a really spirited little passage of windward work. The yacht behaved splendidly, and the seas were at no time too heavy. It is the full-sail breeze that is always a real blessing. Shy winds are tantalising and troublesome, and the harder wind does one no good. It drives the yacht no faster, because we reduce canvas in proportion, and the increased wind merely knocks up a sea which may soon render windward work first unprofitable, and later, perhaps, impossible.

"The distances always look so short on the chart," I was saying. "I'm frankly surprised that we haven't done better than this. She's sailed consistently well, and the seas haven't bothered her a bit. But the tidal stream is almost on the turn now."

We were silent for a while, and I looked musingly across the wind-streaked water towards Cawsand. I looked also at the size of the rollers that were ridging shoreward.

"There'd be a bit of a swell in Cawsand, I fancy," I said to my companion.

"Plymouth then?" he suggested.

I didn't like giving up the idea of Cawsand, because Cawsand would give us a flying start for Fowey next morning. But the idea of a romp up Plymouth Sound, followed by a peaceful night in the Cattewater, was too much of a temptation.

"There's sure to be a swell at Cawsand, and we should probably roll scuppers under," my shipmate observed, as he looked across at the bold outline of Rame Head. "But it's a bit poor to turn tail, I suppose."

"Common-sense," I laughed, "and not turning tail. We've turned tail before now and shall again, but this isn't turning tail at all. Look at the sea; it's all grey and morose and forsaken out here; it begins to look almost dreary. We've had a long day of it, and we don't want more for choice. We're empty and we're tired. We don't want an unquiet night with a chance of dragging. What about a really snug berth behind a stone breakwater and a hot dinner and a long, lazy stretch of one's legs along a cushioned bunk?" "All hands for Plymouth," he echoed cheerily.

Westbound we had rounded Berry Head

We took little interest in Bigbury Bay or Wembury Bay or the Plymouth Mewstone, save as milestones or seamarks on the way. Our one thought was for Plymouth Sound, and for the Cattewater in particular.

There is one submerged rock, the Wells Rock, which makes it inadvisable to prolong one's boards unduly inshore unless its exact position has been established. So we kept well out in the open. The wind was about due west and we were able to make a longish leg each time in the right direction. Yet it seemed very slow. We toppled over the waves, and we wiped the spray out of our eyes, and then we went about. Yes, we were getting well on towards the Mewstone now. Well, Lee ho! once more, and so it went on.

And the Mewstone was equivalent to the desired haven, for there we should be able to ease off the mainsheet a little, and, without again touching a sheet, should fore-reach right up to the Mount Batten breakwater.

Fish, Flesh and Fowl

PORPOISES WERE BREAKING THE SURFACE, in that easy curved rise and dive of theirs. A regular shoal of them were playing, and seagulls were hovering above and dropping continually upon the water, a noisy and raucous swarm. We were sailing in sunshine off Rame Head, and were in Cornish waters.

"Must be a shoal of fish," my shipmate said, "and the porpoises and gulls are both persecuting the unfortunate beggars. It isn't all joy for a fish …

"By Jove, a shark!" He broke off to shout it. "I'm not bathing in this part of the ocean to-day—look at the brute!"

All that was visible of the brute was a triangular dorsal fin, but it was unmistakable; it was cleaving the surface with real purpose like the periscope of a submarine. Being full of courage, with a ten-ton yacht under our feet, we gave chase. The shark seemed to be making away seaward; and, as this brought us off our course, we broke off the chase almost at once, and settled down to serious windward work once more.

"If we were proper sailormen we should have fished for that beggar," my shipmate said, recalling that superstition that a shark's tail brought luck. The old sailing ship would sail the seas with the trophy nailed to her jib-boom. Sometimes the men would have been able to chop the tail off as the greedy brute was being hauled up the ship's side by a half-dozen sturdy fellows. Then the live shark would be dumped overboard, at once to be devoured by his fellow sharks. A pleasant crowd.

It was all very well fishing for sharks with rope tackle from a big ship, but it is a different business altogether to fish for them with rod and line from a boat and play them as one plays a salmon. The latter is a pretty sporting venture. To hook a 300-lb. shark and play him for a couple of hours is something like big-game fishing.

We had now opened Whitesand Bay, with its long line of white sand and brown-grey rock, and we skimmed smoothly onward with easy movement.

We could hear a bell. The tolling note travelled a great distance on a day like this. That was the Knight Errant bell-buoy, marking the outer patch beyond the Sherberterry Rocks.

Polperro

"And there's Looe Island," I said, "as plain as a pike-staff. We're getting on first rate."

The reason why we suddenly noticed the island was that a first gleam of sunlight brought it into clear relief, sharp and snappy against a coastline still in shadow. The sunshine had at last spread to the land, and sun-gleams and cloud-shadows chased one another along the rocky landfalls. Sunlight broke in a flood upon the yacht also, a pleasant glow and warmth. What a perfect passage!

Away sun-ward there was a curious sharp glisten on the water, moving all the time like the crinkle of silver paper. It was fish breaking surface. A shoal of mackerel, surely, and a cloud of gulls above it. It is good fun hunting mackerel under sail; if you can sail through the shoal you are sure of a mackerel on every line. The mackerel were chasing the shoals of tiny brit and sile ('herring-fry' as the fishermen used to call them collectively), and the gulls and bigger fish were chasing them. The mackerel is one of the swiftest fishes that swim. We were inclined to chase this shoal, but it also moved off in the wrong direction.

A little bevy of Looe fishing boats seemed suddenly to spring up about us here. An important fishery is based on Looe, long-lining, drift and trawl. East and West Looe were clearly visible, and also the dip between them where the entrance is. This would be an excellent type of day for entering Looe, but not at this moment, for the tide would be running out, and the tide runs hard. The harbour, furthermore, dries out. We have never entered in a yacht, but have once anchored off shore on a calm day and entered in the dinghy. The bottom of the off-shore anchorage is mud, but in-shore it is clean sand. In quiet weather many little shore boats anchor there to avoid drying out.

The old town that we found was just quays and houses beside the river, and a stone bridge with several arches at the end. Fishing boats were warped alongside the quay walls on both sides, and seagulls flying all round them. My own chief impression of the whole place was of seagulls all round the boats. The quays were picturesque, curving under the shelter of a wooded hill; so were the ships, big luggers, and everything propped up with legs.

We were now off Looe Island, close-hauled still. There are only two houses on it, and neither was visible from here; it looked like a rocky pyramid grassed over on its higher slopes. For persons 'locally acquainted' a channel inshore of the island is available. It can only be used by light craft, of course, and the leading marks are the Dodman just clear of Orestone Rock. The island itself rejoices in various names—it has been known as St. Michael's, St. Nicholas', and St. George's Island, with the result that people have finally solved the difficulty by ignoring the saints altogether and calling it just plain Looe Island. In the days of its sainthood it was much used by smugglers, St. Michael's Chapel itself not being above suspicion.

The long line of the Dodman had been becoming more defined; from a grey blur it had now assumed definite outline; and nearer yet was the Gribbin, with its tall seamark looking rather like a factory chimney. Just this side of Gribbin Head lay the entrance to Fowey.

There were little buoys and spars marking nets all over the place here, and one or two smacks were working to windward like ourselves. Just beyond Looe Island is Orestone Point, and then the Downend shoals, beyond which is Polperro. The wind was very variable; at one moment we had been able to point Gribbin Head, and now we seemed unable to make even Polperro on this tack; but again the breeze freshened and we were making away westward all the time. We could see the houses of Polperro.

There are two stone piers, one behind the other, making an outer and inner harbour; and the tide runs off beyond both of them. The whole place is almost unbelievably picturesque; but, unfortunately for itself, it has become a show place, a beauty spot, like Clovelly.

Squally Weather

WE WERE PEGGING TO WINDWARD, and the wind was a fine full-sail breeze. The yacht was footing it merrily; the seas, though big, were even, and she was sailing so dry that we had no need of oilskins. We had left Fowey, and the sun shone on Gribbin Head.

The glass had been falling a little and the fine weather was too good to last. The low sky was now full of ugly cloud-heads; but these, we thought, meant thunder only and no serious disturbance.

Off Gribbin Head is the Cannis Rock, about a quarter of a mile off-shore. It covers at three-quarters flood and is marked by a red iron pole beacon. We could not see a vestige of the rock itself, but we could see the waves rear themselves as they curled and foamed, and could hear the noise of them. The seas are apt to hit this line of coast pretty strongly; the line of a south-westerly wind is straight from the Lizard.

As we brought Gribbin Head abeam we began to open St. Austell Bay. The day was not improving; obviously, by the look of the clouds, there was heavy rain away to seaward, and rain was falling in a dark and heavy blur over the land also. With us, the sunshine was still brilliant, and it only served to make the skies both to windward and lee look more forbidding. "Thunder somewhere, I suppose," I said, "or we shouldn't have the clouds working along in two directions like that. We'd better have our oilskins handy, or even get into them now, even in this merry sunshine."

161

We made Falmouth, and the lights of the town twinkled

That windward squall was travelling fast. If there were a real burst of wind with it we should have to heave-to and reef at once.

We had scudded along finely on port tack, and we were now looking into St. Austell Bay. The great heaps of waste from the china clay quarries looked like the pyramids of Egypt—big monuments fringed and circled with cloud. The whole impression was rather wonderful. It was a weird picture.

Then the squall hit us. The wind had caught us aback, and we thus found ourselves hove-to, while the rain smote us like fun. It poured in torrents, and the wind whistled, with a vicious note in it. "We shall have to reef," I shouted, "but we'll let this spasm go by. She'll be all right if we keep her hove-to and drop the peak if necessary." Then, after a few minutes of whistling gusts, the wind settled back to the old quarter, still blowing from the south-west, but harder.

Then suddenly the wind had gone.

"Rotten this," my shipmate said, as he began to peel off his oilskins, for the rain by this time was negligible. "Of all the things I loathe at sea I hate this most—

this wallowing helpless with a boom banging and tearing at its sheet, and the ship rolling her guts out, scuppers under. And nothing to do."

"Except to dodge the boom," I suggested, and we grinned.

We had plenty of time to look at this identical coastline. It simply stayed there.

"No fun, no fun," my companion was saying. "D'you think it'll breeze up soon?"

"I have no idea," I admitted. "It's a good job we're well off shore," I yawned.

"More rain," my companion sang out, scrambling aft to seize his oilskin, and sure enough the rain came again, another deluge. It fairly smoked over the water. It streamed on the decks. It poured from our oilskins in solid runlets. Extinguished under our sou'westers we hunched our shoulders and waited for it to finish. It couldn't keep going for long at this pitch.

"Wind." Before the rain was fairly over the wind was upon us. It had freshened once more from the south-south-west, and we kept her sailing close-hauled, and sailing fine also, for fear of heavier gusts.

"This is no fun," I said, and I expect I sounded very querulous, for there is nothing worse than the sense of "waiting for It." And then the breeze did come, not in a sharp gust, but a healthy little breeze, gradually hardening. The sky was lighter and the squall was passing. With a sense of relief we settled down to it, driving merrily forward once more. First rate.

But the breeze was too good to last. It fell away once more, and came again in cats' paws. Then, at long last, the breeze really hardened, and we pulled down a second reef, the yacht pitching heavily over the tops of great green seas while we tied up the reef points. But, the squalls seemed to be over. The sky was brighter; and the yacht, snugged down like this, rode the seas with a beautiful gameness and plugged away to windward with very little fuss. In the late afternoon we made Falmouth, and the lights of the town twinkled.

Port in a Storm

THE SINGING OF BIRDS WAS THE FIRST SOUND that I heard on awakening, then I heard a crowing cock. There was a patter of rain on the cabin roof. Next, while yet barely awake, I was conscious of the soughing of the wind, the *wash-wash* of water against the side of the yacht, and the crying of seagulls. Twin impressions: "This picture and that," I thought drowsily; country and the sea. And on that thought I turned over and fell fast asleep again, very well content to be in haven, here in Helford River, and under no tyrannous need to turn out and make an early departure.

"This is dishonest," my shipmate said later, with one leg out of his bunk as he rose in a dilatory fashion. "When we came in last night with a pocket of wind and a falling glass, I had bargained for a regular gale to-day, so that we could feel all the happier in port. And we've only got a rotten wet day."

It might be a wet day, but it was far from being rotten. Out in the well we stood and enjoyed the soft air and the sweet land scents that from time to time came mingled with the salt breeze. It was a lovely spot at which to awaken. We looked straight out through a narrow opening at the Channel—rather a leaden-looking Channel to-day, I was fain to admit.

And, by the same token, it was none too smooth out there. The wind must still be pretty fresh outside, little as we felt it here. This was a snug spot. The wind was seemingly back in the south-west again, if the clouds were any guide.

We would go out and have a look at it; it was better to get under way than to feel cooped up in here.

We slipped down the river, under double-reefed mainsail, at great speed. Then, when clear of the Gedges, we put her on the wind. We had had no idea that there was so much of it; it almost laid the yacht on her beam ends. Steamers were brought up in the Bay, having evidently run for shelter. This was more than we had bargained for, and we decided to turn tail. We worked cautiously inshore; we were not anxious to pull down another reef, as we should so soon be in shelter again, but we had to handle her carefully. Then there was a long beat up the river, and we were glad to be in.

There was a long beat up the River, and we were glad to be in

The day seemed better near midday, and we went ashore at Helford. We were charmed as ever. The white-walled cottages among the wooded and rocky slopes, the plankbridge and the little creek above which the hillside rose so steeply—all these formed a picture. We left the dinghy and scrambled up the slopes and rambled along the paths. The air was fragrant after the rain, and the luxuriance of the foliage a delight. Higher on the hills we noticed the stone stiles erected to stop the cattle; stone is plentiful and used for everything. We went as far as Manachan Church, which has the fig-tree growing out of the church wall, and we wanted to get a glimpse of Gillan Creek. We spied the water between the stems of the pine trees, and pressed on farther still; then we found the narrow creek and the houses and church by the waterside. The wind was streaking across the water, and there was again a scatter of rain. But we exulted in it all. This was a real West Country mooring, and we were well content.

As we returned to the yacht the dinghy was throwing up spray in sheets, and every indication hinted that we were in for a dirty night. Yes, the barometer was racing down now. The rain (which had been going on most of the afternoon quite unheeded) had recommenced just at the time of the flood, and we had been told ashore that this was a bad sign. We went round every detail on deck with care to see that nothing could get adrift in the night, and then, it being nightfall now, we went below for supper. As we supped we were both nearly thrown off our seats when a heavy gust of wind suddenly hit the yacht and heeled her sharply over for all the world as if she had been under sail. Yes, the fun was beginning.

After a leisurely meal we turned out to look at the night. The clouds were chasing over the sky at great speed, and long lines of foam were streaking the water. Waves were breaking everywhere. And this no doubt was only a beginning. "It's going to be a wild night," I said, "and I only hope that our ground tackle holds." We had already veered out well over thirty fathoms of chain, and had laid out the sturdy little kedge.

We tossed heavily in the night. Oddly enough, I slept like a baby. There was legitimate cause for some worry, because the wind was down the creek, and—if we dragged—we might even drag out to sea, though it was far more likely that we should bring up on the rocks on the north shore. With less provocation I have before now suffered all the pangs of a shipwreck that was never going to happen, and have struggled up on deck every now and then to see if the yacht were really dragging. Unable to gauge this accurately, I have returned to uneasy sleep and hungered for the daylight. But not so to-night. I slept the slumber of childhood, and was only awakened when day was already beginning. "My, what a whack!" I said, as a wave hit the yacht. "I suppose it *is* only a wave," I added, tumbling out of my bunk, and I bustled out in a hurry to see. Yes, it was only a wave; and there seemed to be a good many more like it. The yacht was rocking violently, and sheering about all over the place, but she did not seem to have dragged a particle. So, as the dawn was heavily clouded and the strong wind had a cutting edge, I dropped below again almost as quickly as I had tumbled out. The movement, as felt in the cabin, was a mixture of a roll, a plunge, and a jolt. It became rather less pronounced when the tide turned, and wind and tide were thus in the same direction. But even then the yacht was quite frisky and irrepressible. We lay in our bunks fairly late because there seemed nothing better to do.

Later in the morning we stood in the well and looked out over a waste of foam-capped grey water. "We might just as well go ashore for a stretch," I said. "My one doubt is whether we shall be able to get back on board again." But we decided that we had enough strength and manhood between us for the task, and we went. Down-wind to Helford Point we knew we should be whirled by the wind in a matter of a minute or two; the return passage in the teeth of the gale would be the job that would find us out.

Oil-skinned and sou'westered, we staggered a little on the stable earth as we stepped ashore, although our night voyage had only been on the end of a chain in Helford River. One or two natives joined us and helped us look at the unruly sea. "You can say it's blowin' pretty hard," said one, "when you see steamers bring up in the bay for shelter." We had already noticed that three or four cargo steamers were at anchor outside, and we felt rather glad that they had brought up because of the weather. "And what about that schooner?" I asked, pointing down to a vessel close at hand. "She was here last night, and I think she's dragged a long way, hasn't she?"

"She ha'n't done no good," was the contemptuous answer. "Those fellows, they anchored her there on the grass" (meaning the place where the river bottom is muddy and covered with grass weed). "She's on the rocks already. If the wind holds they'll have a job to pull her off at all."

We returned to the dinghy, and fought our way back on board, an oar each. If we eased for one moment we made sternway in a twinkling, to the undoing of all the work of the last five minutes. And the seas were so short and vicious that the wave-tops kept on giving us a dollop over the bows, until the water was slopping about on the dinghy floor in a lake that swam this way and that with the movement of the boat. There was no chance of baling; if this water bid fair to get us waterlogged, we should have to turn tail and run ashore.

We were honestly glad to be back on board again. As always, the yacht seemed to be so big and solid and stable, after the bobbing and wallowing dinghy. And the cabin was warm and snug; here we were—this was 'port in a storm.'

Going as Crew

M Y EDUCATION HAS BEEN NEGLECTED. It all comes of being such a half-taught amateur, for I have always done as I liked.

When sailing with a skipper who really knows his business (though an amateur also) it is quite different, and the guest (if he is a sailing man himself) will feel that he has got to toe the line. In the cabin he is an honoured guest, and may be attentively waited on and considered with every solicitude; but on deck (if he knows what's what) he is under orders. True, the skipper does not claim the scornful isolation of the ordinary shipmaster; he may quite often ask one's opinion, but it is not for the crew to offer an opinion unasked. The crew awaits the order, and then jumps to it.

The skipper and I came down from town together and joined the yacht (a 27-ton ketch) in the Cattewater at Plymouth. One paid hand was employed. He met us at the station, carried our traps, put us on board, and girded himself and served us at table in the warm and well-lit cabin, while the yacht rolled perpetually to the wash of the ferry steamers.

The morning that followed was grey and looked unsettled, but the wind was very light. We were up at five and made sail. I turned to with a will. "If you haven't got a spike," said the skipper in his gentlest tone, "there's one on the port side shelf in the cabin." And two things were at once clear to me: (1) that I hadn't got a spike, and (2) that, if I had turned up with a spike duly dangling at the end of a lanyard I should have cut a more seamanlike figure.

It was a wretched morning: there was a drizzle in the air. The yacht plugged down to the breakwater under auxiliary power and we hoped to pick up a breeze outside. All that we picked up was a heavy swell. The waves were smooth-surfaced, but large. And the engine chugged and the yacht rolled. I was at the wheel. "West by South," the skipper said to me. "West by South, Sir," said I.

Then, off Rame Head, the engine suddenly packed up. Here was a job for the hand? Not a bit of it. The skipper had pounced on it himself like a tiger. The hand stood by and held things. The skipper cleaned the carburetter, and emptied the tank and refiltered the petrol back into it. And all the time the yacht rolled helplessly; and I sat at the wheel with a wise air but disabled, looking for a breeze.

It was not until noon (the engine being now in order) that we picked up a breeze and began really to sail. The engine was shut off with joy, and the yacht herself revelled. This was a beam wind, and she cut a white swath through the water. And so we made Helford River, where we brought up after sunset.

For the return passage we were again stirring at five in the morning. The wind was light at the moment; but the day was a day of 'squalls.' The skipper wanted petrol and he decided to put into Falmouth to replenish. Away under sail, with a westerly breeze, we were soon at sea. "We can strike the topsail in a moment if need be," the skipper decided, and the jib header was sent up. The first squall hit us just before Falmouth entrance, where we should have had to hand the topsail anyway. And down it came.

I was kept at the wheel, and we turned the yacht up the harbour towards Flushing. Dark skies, a stiff breeze, and streaming oilskins. A message was conveyed ashore by a motor boat to send petrol off to us. And, in the meantime, I at the wheel was ordered to stand off and on, or in other words, to hang about. When a nasty job like that is assigned, one is told that one is 'the best helmsman.' With a stiff wind, a sluicing tide, and a medley of shipping, it was frankly hateful. I disliked the *Cutty Sark* (then moored at Falmouth), I hated every vessel in the anchorage. And when I had to make the yacht beat to and fro with a boat lashed alongside, and the owner more interested in the petrol funnel than in the fate of his own topsides and bowsprit, I hated the whole job still worse. I criss-crossed that harbour till further notice, and I don't want to do it again. But at last the boat was paid off and we were free. It was a joy to be on an honest course once more. A brown-sailed cutter yacht with two reefs down accompanied us out, neck and neck; but once outside the harbour the stronger wind and our greater waterline length told, and we sailed away from her. She, moreover, shaped course coastwise for Fowey, and we stood away on a compass course for Bolt Head.

The skipper was a tiger for work, and he revelled in sail shifting. He took me into his counsels now. "Shall I reset the topsail?" he queried.

"There's a lot of weight in the squalls," I ventured. "Look at it, that's a pretty dirty squall coming." With a rueful look he accepted the view. "Why not the squares'l?" he added with a chuckle. "Come on, we'll get the squares'l ready." He made himself thoroughly happy by getting everything prepared, and he did

The brown-sailed cutter yacht with two reefs down accompanied us out

twice as much as the hand, though the latter was both willing and skilful, but no squares'l was set. The wind piped up too much after all, and the sail was unbent and sent back to the locker.

I was still at the wheel and I confess that all my deviations from my compass course were towards luffing. Loss of a few miles was nothing; an accidental gybe might be serious. I remember reading of a racing helmsman who said: "I would never feel the same to myself if I had an accidental gybe." Rot, says I. When you are handling a yacht that sheers about as wildly as this or any yacht does in these big following seas there's no holding her. If you try to sail her true on course with a wind dead aft—well, some day or other you'll be found out. But I watched my lubber line each time I saw that the owner was coming aft!

We were miles out to sea as we crossed that big bay upon which Plymouth stands, and the wind was stronger still. We had to change jibs. The skipper for once took the wheel. "Go for'ard and give a hand," he ordered me.

The yacht was pitching handsomely, and I had to clamber deftly and hold tight. The view from beside the bitt-heads was magnificent, with miles upon miles of that great rolling sea, and the Bolt Tail, fringed with white foam, jutting into it. Then, the work done, I crawled aft, and gradually we closed that iron coast. The spray was being flung half-way up the cliff at times. One likes to feel sure that all the gear is first class with a shore like that so close aboard!

A cold windy twilight was on us before we rounded the Start, with its jagged little outliers of rock. Once round it, the sea smoothed as if by magic. We were bound for Dartmouth.

Night had fallen now. The skipper had gone below, and I had been told to steer a course for the lighted buoy. That course was too far off shore, but we were soon able to luff up and bring the harbour lights in line. Then—after a flattering consultation with me—we brought up off Kingswear Castle, at the pilots' mooring, which I knew so well.

In the night we rocked and rolled gently. A steamer's foghorn in the small hours was simply a roar and a bellow right beside us. Gratefully I turned over in my warm bunk; why worry? I need not bother, because (a) I was only 'crew,' and so it was no business of mine to turn out unless summoned, and (b) I knew we had anchored in the red sector out of the fairway, and that this was good holding ground.

We entered Dartmouth at dawn, and I got my discharge, with a first-class character, I believe. But I doubt whether I had deserved it.

My Yachting Cap

A LL CONVENTION CAN BE FLUNG to the four winds the moment a cruising yacht is well off-shore. In the old days some of us (when we were the penniless cruising men of the East Coast in happy times) were content with any old clothes; and we would never wear the yachting cap. On the contrary, we regarded as suspect the people who did. Sometimes, and often with reason, we used to get out our fenders when we saw a crew of white cap-covers beating into a small East Coast anchorage. For ourselves, we had no time for the fripperies of dress; and we were not the idle rich.

Since then, times have changed, and the regulation yachting cap is met with even in the smallest of cruising yachts. I wear it myself. But am I promoted in public esteem by this badge of yachtsmanship, as I ought to be? Not a bit of it. I am not drawing upon imagination; the little incidents that I record belong to actual fact.

Swanage Bay is a good place to bring up in during south-westerly winds; it is rather more 'roily' than Studland, but the shelter is excellent. I went ashore for a spell, in well-creased grey bags (one can't run to white for ordinary cruising; they don't stay white long enough), blue jacket, and yachting cap—quite looking the part. As I gazed out at the little white yacht in the Bay, perhaps I felt the glow of satisfaction that most of us feel when we look at our little ships at anchor—until I was awakened by a loud voice across the road, in a north-country burr: "Here, Hi! When does the next steamer start for Bournemouth?"

It was only left to me to confess ignorance, look pleased about the little incident—and decamp.

But this is only a beginning. Suppose, at the home port, you keep the car handy for little errands, and, seizing the only cap that is lying about in the cabin, you go ashore. Before you have driven half a dozen miles inland the dashing yachtsman has become the dandy chauffeur. On one occasion, when I was cooling my heels while my shipmate was in a shop, a fellow chauffeur was inclined to be quite chatty and pleasant about things in general.

Another time I was ashore at Plymouth with a friend both wearing yachting caps. We were walking up a by-street, and some youngsters were just passing us. One small boy stepped in front and pointed a finger at each of us in turn.

"*He's* a busman," said the child, "and *he's* a busman." The child knew a busman when he saw one, just as he knew a horse or a motor car.

"Yes, and if you're not good we won't give you a ride in the bus," my shipmate told him. The child gave one look of respect and admiration, and then scuttled off and joined his companions.

My next character was that of a harbour-master or waterman, I am not sure which. It was at Cowes (and, of course, if one rowed one's own dinghy about during a pre-war Cowes Week such little happenings might be expected, because the thing was simply not done in polite circles).

I received an abrupt hail from a smart yacht: "Can you show us to a berth up here?"

I couldn't, I was afraid—even for a consideration; but I rested on my oars and gave such information as I possessed.

Then at Torquay I had occasion to go for a short ride on a tram while shopping—when there were still tramcars in Torquay. I was obviously a passenger, but I suppose that a tram conductor even off duty ought to be a mine of information. As I rose to leave the tram a detaining hand fell upon my arm:

"Does this tram go to —?" asked an old gentleman.

I had never heard of the place, but I had to be civil and helpful about it, or he might have reported me to the company.

Lamentable, is it not? And yet, believe me, I knew a fellow who simply would not go ashore with you from his own yacht if you were wearing a yachting cap. He used to say that it always meant that the shop people put up their prices when they saw you coming. Little did he know. I must procure from somewhere a conductor's badge for him to wear on his manly breast, and that badge—in conjunction with the regulation cap—ought surely to bring the prices down instead. I really don't know; and perhaps on the whole it will be better to leave things as they are.

PART III

Those Happier Days

When We Were Young

THE FIRST TEN YEARS of this present century are now worlds away. Then England had waged no war in western Europe for some ninety years, and no one alive had any experience of such calamities. England was rich and prosperous. We used to walk about with golden sovereigns and half sovereigns in our pockets. We could get a ginger beer for one penny, and draught of real beer for a couple of pence. And fact it is that, when I first enjoyed sailing in open boats on Blackwater, I was able to get accommodation, perfectly clean, and food, good and ample, for 14s. a week! That world is worlds away.

And of course I was young. Of the happy days on those tidal waters I have no logs, and there was really nothing worth recording in that 'messing about with small boats.' Sunlit day and day of squall were merry alike. Those days were good; and they are gone.

My shipmate and I slept ashore for the most part, but in the boat we carried a tarpaulin of Willesden canvas, under which we could sleep. Our usual routine on those occasions was to don our oilskins and to lie down on the bare boards, one of us on each side of the centreboard case. We had cushions for our heads, but no other luxury. And we slept like tops.

The recollections of those happy days are still a joy, but they are no material for stories. On paper they are dull. It is the mischances that make the tale, few though they are, as against the many jaunts that prospered.

And here is such a case of mischances.

One Snowy Night

IN LONDON IT WAS SNOWING HARD on a day in early March.

"Week-ending?" an elderly friend said, with a glance at my kit-bag, as I entered his office.

"Just off—sailing," I explained.

He guffawed. He looked out at the driving snow, he looked at the fire in his own hearth, and he shrugged his shoulders.

"Each to his choice," he said, and glanced back affectionately at the red flames. "Well, get on with it, you young ass. Good luck."

In the perfect spirits of youth I bundled off to Liverpool Street, and was glad that the train was punctual at Maldon because I knew that my margin of tide was narrow. But I found Maldon looking like a Christmas card, the streets deep in snow and the roofs fairly piled with it. "Good job I've got my sea-boots on," I thought as I shuffled heavily through the deserted streets. The snow was driving in from the north-east in a cloud that blinded, and people had been driven indoors. Firelight shone through the casements of the old houses.

The little boat was kept on the beach at Maldon, and I shouldn't be long. I intended to sleep ashore—at Osea or Steeple Stone. So I shuffled on through the snow. I could barely keep my eyes open as I faced this hurricane of whirling flakes. Yes, I'd do like other people to-night, and have a stick of fire in the grate when I got there. What a day!

The beach was deserted, and the tide falling fast. I eyed it with concern and hastened my steps, for the tide forsakes Maldon altogether. There was hammering in the boat-shed, and—as I turned in to get my oilskins—my boatman friend looked up from his job.

"Wonnerful bad weather. Disappointing, that is," he said.

Then he saw me getting my oilskins off the pegs.

"What, you're not starting?" he said. "You don't mean to go?"

I had an old overcoat there; I put it on, under the oilskins, and tramped off, solitary.

Snow was heaped upon all the boats on the beach, and the tide-water—murky grey in contrast with the whiteness—gurgled greedily seaward. There was no time to lose.

I stripped off the cover. Snow, intrusive always, had managed to percolate inside. How it does it I have no idea. The cover had been taut as a drum from coaming to coaming, but none the less the thin white layer was there inside.

I stepped the mast, tied up one reef in the mainsail, and was away. Making short boards, I worked down the fairway, smothered in snow. I frankly enjoyed it. The snowflakes, drifting thickly, coated the sail at once and turned its warm brown colour white. Lee ho! The sail swung inboard and shook violently, scat-

I found Maldon looking like a Christmas card

tering all that coat of snow *into the boat*. It did it every time. The other side of the sail was coated in a moment, and then—lee ho!—again it deposited the whole consignment into the boat and spread itself out for more.

The wind was searching. I would have minded less if I could have stood up to steer and could have beaten my feet on the floorboards of the well of a yacht; but I had to sit. The snow smothered me, and the tide was getting low; I felt the centre-board touch once as she went about.

There is a narrow channel to Osea, and the mud was still just covered. Night was coming on, and everything to eastward was one blur of cloud and driving snow. Not a thing was visible. After beating for a short distance, I capitulated. I turned and ran back; I would land at Heybridge Basin, sleep ashore there, and be away with to-morrow's ebb at dawn. That would have to do.

Then, at that very moment, as ill-luck would have it, the snowfall stopped as if by magic. The whole winter-world was crystal-clear in the grey light. The long line of Osea Island was there, the buoys and leading marks were all visible. Every difficulty had gone.

179

The change at the moment had a genial appearance, as of smiling fortune. I chuckled. Not so bad, after all; I should manage it. The boat was round in a moment and I was beating seaward, exhilarated. The tide was falling fast, but I should just do it. First rate!

On I went, skirting the shore of Northey Island and down to Clark's Buoy. Then the thing happened. The world in a moment vanished from sight in a scurry of whirling snow-flakes, and night had fallen. The sudden deepening of clouds and the sudden snow brought nightfall in one instant; it was just as Coleridge said: "At one stride comes the dark."

Perhaps it was not only the trickle of snow down my neck that sent a shiver down me. Night out here was remarkably ungenial. Then the centre-board touched, and then it scraped again; no, I hadn't a single dog's chance of finding my way to Osea through this misery of driving snow. I remember I watched the silly stuff with a touch of contempt because it kept going the wrong way, and—for quite long periods—the idiotic flakes were whirling upwards in one long drift instead of coming down. The flakes were not snow-white now, but dark specks, and the cold was detestable. I had no fancy at all for a night out here; and oh! for a warm bed! Con-*found* that clearing! Why the Dickens hadn't I done the sensible thing and gone ashore at Heybridge Basin? Anyhow, I'd follow the wise plan now. I let her run.

Then scrape, scrape, even in mid-channel. At all events, the centre-board was serving no earthly purpose now; up with it. Here was I, in a stretch of tidal water a mere half-mile wide, which was shallowing to a depth of a couple of feet, and narrowing to a trickle; and here was I, marooned in it almost, for—hang it all, she was brought up, dead.

Through the darkness I could see the wink of one light ashore—at the window, no doubt, of some cheerful room. And if this *verdammte* boat were determined to ground in the fairway, I could not very well leave her, for the riding light lay in the boathouse, and the tide here would be up again before dawn. Well, there it was, I must get out and shove her. The water would top my sea-boots, and off they came, and I rolled my breeches above my knees. Ugh! but the water was cold. The boat, relieved of my weight, floated, and I turned her toward that kindly light. Then the boat scraped and brought up, immovable.

Slowly I got on board again, and put on my considering cap. Item one, the snow had got through my oilskin and overcoat, and my clothes were sodden. Item two, this boat was as wet as a half-filled bath. Item three, this snow seemed interminable, and the wind was cutting. Item four, that light betokened something which was very heaven's own self. Yes, I'd get ashore somehow. As soon as the flood-tide came up in the night, I'd put off in a dinghy and fetch her; but, in the meantime—a meal—a fire—even a doze. Yes!

With decision I stepped over the side, and, after driving the fluke of the anchor soundly home, I was soon flop, flop, flopping in slow and clumsy progress over the mud. I did not know the lay of the tidal flats as I know it now, and I shaped (as I afterwards saw) the very worst course over the very softest mud; and the snow came more ghostly and full than ever, quenching even the one star of light.

In hope of a change ashore into dry clothing, I was carting along a bag with me. The bag was a mistake. I floundered heavily. Anyone with experience of walking through soft mud knows how any weight at all is a handicap, for the whole thing is a matter of balance. If the poise is thrown out of the true, one cannot hold up. Flop! right down in the mud I went.

The slough seemed oozier and oozier. I could not keep the bag above the mud, so that both the bag and I were getting lavishly decorated; and then I brought up, absolutely winded.

Never in my life have I felt so utterly solitary; solitude in a seaway or an open moor is nothing to it. The drifting snow was wraith-like, and the mud like the slime of a bottomless pit. I was lost. The night was without a glimmer—utter, homeless, primeval, sobbing darkness. And I felt suddenly afraid; I do not attempt to disguise it—I was really afraid.

I had heard of soft spots in mud which will swallow a man and leave no trace— perhaps I should strike one. And even if not, I despaired of reaching the shore through acres of this unholy slime; it simply couldn't be done, I was dead-beat. The despised amenities of my forsaken little ship would be a godsend now, could I but find it. I must try to return in my own tracks, for otherwise… well, I fancied. The tide would return and cover me, for I never could extricate myself if the tide in the darkness were upon me.

Heybridge Basin was a picture in the sun

These were the images that lurked in background of a tired brain as I floundered and sprawled. Then I missed my tracks and was fairly lost. Yes, there was no mistake about it, I was afraid.

Slosh, slosh, slosh, I went on blindfold through the mud, shaping a course by instinct rather than knowledge, for I could see nothing. I began to think I should be dead before morning. At long last a thinning of the snow brought a glimmer of greyness, a faint relief of the unutterable black. There, not far away, loomed the dark shape of something material. Yes, it was the boat. I squash-squash-squashed through the sludge, and fairly flung myself upon it before the darkness snatched it from sight again; for the feel of something hard and stationary was a blessed contrast to the sliding horror of that intolerable slime.

I would now do my best—not perhaps for comfort—but at least to minimise the abject squalor of it; and the relief from the spectre of that evil mud was a luxury in itself. The snow gave over, but the Arctic wind drove right through one: it was bitter, searching to the marrow. Everything reeked with snow, but I stretched the cover over the boat, wetness and all, lashed it down, and then crept in, out of the wind at all events.

Out of the wind? Yes, I had thought so, and yet it probed and wormed its way in somehow, getting through everything. My teeth chattered in my head, and I rolled the sodden mainsail round me in hope of a little bit of heat. Often enough before, I had lain down on the floorboards by the centre-board case, fully dressed, and had slept the whole night through, unwakening; but to-night sleep evaded me entirely. I heard the wind moaning over the flats, I heard it hit the boat as she lay there immovable, and I heard it whistle away into distance again. It made the canvas cover slat, it whined through the little shrouds and halliards, it buffeted the hull. Its sighing sound was a continual tune. Once or twice I looked out: all the world was one blur of darkness.

Then a new sound awakened. Lap, lap, lap, I could hear the water. I could fancy it, for the rising tide has a wonderful fascination, and I have watched it spellbound times without number, brimming in, searching its way in little trickles and rivulets, drowning the mud. To-night I could *hear* it. It was wind-creased into little wavelets I knew; they lap, lap, lapped, breaking their puny little crests against the stranded hull.

She was soon afloat, and I began to keep watch, in case some barge, careering up through the darkness, might run down my unlighted boat. But nothing came, nothing except—at long last—the dawn.

A handful of stars had sometimes glimpsed for a moment and then gone again, behind the driving night-wrack. Clouds were now racing across a sullen red dawn. I found myself afloat in a small seaway, covered with breaking waves, for the tide was high, and long before the sun was up the tide had turned.

I began to get busy. I stripped off the cover, now stiff with frost. The wind was due north this morning, and I should romp down to Osea. Up went the sail, and away the little boat flew. Heybridge Basin and Mill Beach were a picture in the snow, but I saw nothing after I had made sail. She was over-canvased and inclined to steer wildly, but away she flew. I felt numb from the hips downward, but the uplift and elation of that flying sail in the snowy dawn I shall never forget. Even if feet and hands were benumbed and blue, this warmed the cockles of my heart. It was splendid.

Off Osea Pier I anchored and went ashore, just to stamp up and down and restore the feeling to my limbs. It was not until three hours later that I was able to get the hot breakfast and stiff grog which put me in tune with the whole universe. Though rather inclined to nod and drop asleep by the fire, I roused and kicked myself out of doors. A day's holiday must not be squandered.

I was back at Maldon with the afternoon tide. That wind was as cold as ever; but by the waterside I still loitered, fascinated. I watched the tide ebb away in the frosty twilight and the night follow. With a sigh I turned to catch the last train to town.

Hunting the Weather Shore

I

MUCH DEPENDS UPON ONE'S COMPANION. Had my old shipmate been with me, true yoke-fellow and sharer of fortune's every whim, the first and only preoccupation had certainly been to get the sails up and the mooring-buoy overboard, were it morning, noon or night. When, on the other hand, I am greatly honoured, as now, and my wife is my sailing companion, the first item is an inspection; she must ascertain whether (for example) there are clean newspapers on the shelves of the grocery locker.

When a sailing man has his wife for shipmate, it behoves him to be careful, *if that wife is not herself a sailing woman.* This is my predicament, and if perhaps, from my showing, my companion is not invariably sufficient for these things, the explanation is simple. She does not covet proficiency. Our outlooks on this particular matter are not completely harmonised. There was a well-known artist who went to the East to paint portraits of Arab chieftains. The chiefs were impressed by his skill, but deemed it a contemptible form of cleverness, a case of ingenuity misdirected. That exactly represents the manner in which my present shipmate regards the technique of yachtsmanship. It may have its uses for some people, but she is not one of them; she does *not* aspire to its laurels. She looks on with tolerant indifference, slightly amused. My lady is happy to share and to patronise my pursuit, provided that she is not pressed to accompany me too frequently; she is warmly appreciative of the changes of scene, she approves the expeditions ashore, she revels in the sunlit beaches and the freedom. But the sailing? The sailing is the one drawback.

I had rowed her out in the dinghy across the narrow strip of ruffled blue water, and we had boarded the yacht in the afternoon sunlight. I am always thrilled just a trifle, when I thus return, by the sight of the little hooker. So meek and docile an object she is, as she lies at her mooring in the quiet water, and so utterly different—a tethered captive—from her other self under the moods and changes of wind and sea. Full-sailed, she has wandered coastwise, shimmering in the sunshine; close-reefed, she has thrashed to windward in squall and shower whither she would; baffled and with torn canvas, she has run staggering before the gale whither she would not. And here, at her mooring, she lies again, just as mild and as quiet as if she had never been anywhere in all her life. In her every mood, in her tameness or her activity, she seems surely to be other than mere wood and iron and canvas; personality she has, and why not soul? All of which is, of course, quite irrelevant to the subject in hand.

So here we were on board, and the usual tour of inspection had commenced. I, if I discharged my role with becoming humility, should stand at attention, and (like Artemis prologuising)

Await, in fitting silence, the event,

but I am afraid that I sometimes forget myself to the extent of a wide and private grin.

For I am prepared for what will follow. And it is, moreover, held no treason on my part if I season my homage with mockery. Else, indeed, I had never dared to put pen to paper in this matter.

"Do you *never* put clean papers on the lockers? You were down here only last week."

"Well, when sometimes there isn't any wind... It fell off entirely at the Mid-Barrow at about twelve on Friday night, but then we seized the opportunity to cook some bacon and eggs, because we hadn't had anything since lunch, and I had forgotten to bring the meat."

"But you were anchored or something next day." My inquisitor follows it, as one who presses an advantage.

"Dover inner harbour. But then we slept all the afternoon, until the Customs man woke us up to ask for one and fivepence-halfpenny harbour dues."

"What's this great stain on the red cushion?" The ground of attack is shifted.

"It was shoved in to keep the jam-jars and things from rolling about in the locker, and the condensed milk capsized on it somehow."

She is not appeased. "It's not the least use your having good things," she asserts, "when you only spoil them like this."

There was a blue sky somewhere outside this little hive of a cabin, and a fresh breeze driving white masses of cloud across it, but these matters were matters of no moment. We were busy.

Finally, however, I was released to go on deck and bend the sails, while more serious work continued in the cabin below. I pottered happily about my job, there being an ample margin of tide, and I worked like the British workman. The British workman lays one brick with leisurely precision, and then gazes round upon the spacious prospect, getting strength after a decent and very considerable interval to push the next brick into position. I on my side tied up one mousing, and then I paused in sheer enjoyment of the blue water stretching seaward, and the sunlit world in general; then, after a pensive interval, I went to the length of screwing up the shackle at the clew of the fores'l and leading the sheets aft. At that point a flushed face emerged from the cabin into the sunlight, hair was tossed back with a deft shake, and my inspection below was invited. I went below.

"*Isn't* that different?"

Now I can never tell from the mere appearance of things whether the general post is 'half done' or 'done.' I have been unwarily caught in that manner before. I once said how nice and tidy it looked when I was supposed to say just the opposite, to bear witness, indeed, to its horrible confusion before the tidying had begun. Therefore, after agreeing that it is different, I now do one of two things. Either I await a hint as to whether I am expected to praise or to revile, or (more probably) I fade away into the open air again.

We were now ready to get under way. We have sailed hundreds of miles together, but I am credibly informed that sailing is "rather a waste of time." When in fact we are sailing, the moment is deemed appropriate for reading or sleeping, or for otherwise killing time until the anchor is dropped overboard and the dinghy manned for the shore. There is one exception, which works on a sliding scale. If the water is so rough as to interfere with the colour and atmosphere of the story-book, then the hand that rocks the cradle comes forth and rules the tiller.

"I only do this to keep my mind off it," she asserts with austerity, in case I should think that sailing is a matter of free choice with her.

'It' is not the tiller, nor the story-book, but... well, it is a certain undesired contingency, not unknown upon the unquiet ocean.

Sometimes 'it' becomes a little assertive, and the tiller may even be relinquished, the novel being also at a severe discount. At that stage I am invoked to hunt the weather-shore.

I am, however, anticipating. Time was gradually slipping away; and, as we should dry out if we remained at the mooring, I suggested that we must shift. From my partner, preoccupied with household affairs, I obtained concurrence, but her concurrence was without enthusiasm. She shook out the duster.

"Well, if we must go, go somewhere where we shan't lob about. I can't stand that lobbing."

This injunction, though in somewhat untechnical language, conveys my first order to find the weather-shore. And that for the next ten days will be my main preoccupation, because sailing is (on good authority) 'rather a waste of time,' whereas a comfortable anchorage, where reading and writing can conveniently be done, is the *summum bonum* of a little cruise of ten days' duration.

A second order, crisp and decided as the first, followed on its heels.

"We won't go far. There's still a lot to do, and then there's the dinner to cook."

"Then down with all this rubbish below. Here it comes."

Reigning over the cabin, my sailing companion puts out on deck anything that vexes her sight in that nether domain. I, on the other hand, insist on 'decks cleared for action;' anything that does not properly belong on deck is hurled below. There are protests. After mutual observations, the matter is generally compromised by putting every unfriended article into the long-suffering fo'c'sle.

"Not far, remember; it's getting late already."

It was a golden afternoon. The sunlight touched everything with a singular mellowness; everything was coloured, but everything was harmonious. The water was rippled blue, and the gulls, sailing and curving above us, were now in sunlight, now in shadow.

The wind being westerly, the hunt for the weather-shore should not be a difficult effort. Northey Island would give us ample shelter if we 'let go' above the Doubles buoys, just far enough down to avoid drying. This would be less than a couple of miles away, and thither we accordingly repaired.

I then made myself exceedingly useful at emptying the dust-pan and explaining the use and value of many objects which my lady thought suitable for a watery grave. The fid was one of them.

"It isn't a screwdriver or a gimlet; and, anyhow, it's quite blunt and can't be of any use."

My lecture given on marlinspike seamanship was not very adequate, but it sufficed to confuse the inquirer and so to effect the fid's reprieve; and the suggestion that I should set the primus stoves going was accepted with favour. I settled myself down at the cooking galley as one who finds himself at home again. At all events (as I had the politeness to state), I would rather cook the dinner than spend my time pulling the contents of the lockers out and then putting them back again, even if I did call the process 'tidying.' It was a gross libel upon her deft handiwork, but quite harmless—as harmless, in fact, as the ball of whipping twine which came flying at my head, but (needless to mention) missed it.

So here we were, anchored above Osea Island in the Blackwater estuary. I felt that I had fairly captured my quarry on this occasion; my weather-shore was secure beyond a peradventure. Even if the weather disimproved, we should not suffer greatly, for that would surely mean that the wind had backed to the south-west. Wind would be across tide, and would knock up no sea. If wind veered to north-west, it would probably mean finer weather and less breeze. So I sat on the cabin-top, well pleased with my own weather-wisdom. I had scored this time.

My shipmate was now out beside me, pleased with the blue estuary and the sunshine. We were well content, with the wide sky over us, while the ebb tide that sluiced by was gradually uncovering the spacious mudbanks. These banks, at low tide, would draw quite close to us, but we should float in deep water. As they uncovered, the seagulls began to haunt them, dropping with hoarse cries upon obscure morsels of food, or busying themselves in little white groups and splashing through the pools. Herons were also there, standing at the shallow edge of the water, or, at long intervals, spreading their dark wings and changing their fishing

Irene

ground. The banks were full of quiet colour, and every pool and stream gave back the deep blue of the sky. In an almost windless atmosphere there was a sense of very peace itself; the only sounds beside the changing voices of the gulls were the sound of the water emptying from the flats into the creeks and fleets, and the ripple of the ebb, parted by the bows of the yacht.

The sun was well down toward the western horizon, where it met with a deep cloudbank. The cloud prevailed. Although pouring floods of golden light over its edges, the sun went down unseen. The great cloud built itself into a solid mountain and a deep-toned roll of sound reverberated over the wide, flat landscape, and seemed to be echoed back from the opposite horizon. Thunder.

Now not the least pleasant part of an idle cruise is this intimacy with Nature. One can experience this more fully when at anchor and in indolence, than when busy at the tiller. Here were we in a great solitude, with the wide distances around us, and nothing to do but to watch the march of the storm. There was immediate retreat available to the cabin as soon as it should break. Meanwhile we could see and enjoy the might of the cloud-boulders, with their long festoons of sweeping rain etched in grey lines below them; and, on the other horizon, the retreating golden day, with sunlight still full-coloured upon the far-distant landscape.

"Can't you get the washing-up finished before that storm comes on?"

The voice at my elbow reminded me that when I said I had 'nothing to do,' I had really meant that I was not doing it. I had the mop in one hand and a dirty plate in the other, while I was gazing at 'cloud towers by ghostly masons wrought.' In chastened mood, I scoured the cups and plates.

Now he who 'hunts the weather-shore' has little use for thunder. It is a disturbing element, and has a habit of changing the most excellent weather-shore into a lee shore without previous notice. Being responsible to maintain the stability of the ship's keel, I was rather anxious now to know what was coming. One or two vicious catspaws caused the yacht to snub quite savagely at her cable, but as the thunder died away these sudden draughts died also, and I was able to claim credit for her log-like sobriety when I put up the riding light a little later.

She lay stock still. The grey water was hardly ruffled, and there was a mist with the deep twilight after the heavy rain which had fallen. Later still, the dull grey scene was windless, and the water was like oil.

"So to bed," as Pepys used to say. We slept in the perfect calm. I, for one, dozed off comfortably, stirred and stretched luxuriously in the warmth, and dozed off again, and then fell into sound and heavy sleep. Perhaps I dreamed later. At all events, some malign influence seemed to have bewitched my bedroom; the walls were no longer upright, but were dancing somehow. Oddly, too, my own body appeared to be involved in the antics. I opened my eyes with a start. Grey morning light was in the cabin, and the cabin was performing a most remarkable combination of upending and side-stepping, while a howling wind was driving rain that lashed the cabin-top like a flail. What an awakening! What a life! What a world!

As if the noise outside were not sufficient, a deep groan issued from the opposite bunk. An upheaval of blankets arose and subsided, followed by a queer sound, part sigh, part sneeze. Then a peculiarly thin and desolate voice spoke:

"Can't we get out of this?"

We certainly could 'get out,' on deck, for instance, or into the dinghy, but we should only get wet through. The iron had not yet entered into my soul, and it was on the tip of my tongue to make some such foolish remark, but I wisely suppressed it. My companion would have been in no mood for nonsense. I went out to look at the aspect of things instead.

It was exactly what I might have expected. The wind was north-westerly, blowing straight down the channel against the tide. My vaunted weather-shore had ceased to exist. I rubbed the rain out of my eyes with the wet sleeve of the oilskin, and looked at the prospect. Rather, perhaps, I looked where the prospect ought to have been, for view there was none. Everything was blotted out by the rain. What little *could* be seen was hardly worth looking at. The waves were steep, pitted all over with the quick splashes of the rain. Almost every wave curled and foamed with a sort of ill-temper. The yacht bobbed and dipped and splashed, and then, by way of variety, she would suddenly give a mighty lurch which nearly threw one over. If anybody thinks that no 'sea' is encountered in these tidal estuaries, let him anchor here when a strong north-wester is blowing *down* the channel, and a healthy spring tide is running full tilt *up* it. He will soon know better.

We certainly would 'get out of this,' and the sooner we moved the better for us. This anchorage was no place for to-day. My wretched weather-shore being defunct, a successor must be found. Of stern necessity I know them by heart, and I returned to the cabin with an assumed air of alacrity and cheerfulness.

"We will shift down to the other end of Osea," I said; "we shall be perfectly snug there."

I had hoped that this announcement of immediate action would be well received, but I suffered disappointment. The blankets heaved rebelliously, and there was no response at all. That, from experience, I knew to be a bad sign. I had to repeat my proposed line of action, but the confident tone had left it, I had scented opposition.

An arm came out, and was flopped sternly on the rug. Then a voice sounded from somewhere low down, the resolution of which put my own completely into the shade.

"No, we'll go back to the mooring. *The thing does stand still there at least part of the time*"

The 'thing' thus slightingly referred to was the yacht, and it was evidently not in very high favour just now. Clearly the debate was closed. The arm went back and the figure rolled over on its side and took no further notice.

And I know far better than to thwart my sailing companion in the earliest stage of a little cruise. A critical period has to be endured before she is acclimatised to her surroundings. Her fancy for the mooring was due to the fact that the yacht dries out at low water there, and then it is that 'the thing does stand still for at least part of the time.' The keel is not sharp, and the mud is soft; the yacht therefore lies as nearly upright as may be.

Seeing that, with this wind, we should have a weather-shore when afloat, I could raise no objection on that account. My main objection was one of sheer laziness. Osea could be reached under headsails only, but it would be needful to tie up a couple of reefs for turning to windward, which seemed a waste of energy to sail a mile or so.

I mentioned this, and the figure found that it was not, after all, asleep. It rolled over and took notice. As I was ready to move, I was again a person fit to talk to. My counsels were even promoted by a useful suggestion of her own.

"Why can't you go up with one sail only, like you did yesterday?"

I think I shall never convince her that we should not be very successful at turning to windward under jib only. But, in her opinion, we ought to.

My lady, like the rest of us, is full of contradictions. She has no fancy for sailing, and yet she is really an expert helmswoman; turning to windward (when the sails have been set according to *my* ideas rather than *hers*), she can be trusted to squeeze the very last bit of progress out of every board. When reaching or running free she is in favour of rather too straightforward methods. She has, moreover, an idea that shoals of which I warn her have somehow been put there just to annoy her, and that I am in some obscure manner responsible.

"It would be much better if we kept straight on," says she; and when I say that we must gybe, my partner thinks it's nonsense. "She's going so nicely like this," she observes, "it seems a pity to disturb her." After the gybe, I am liable to condemnation because, on a hot day, the mainsail is no longer acting as a sunshade for her, and on a cold day, because I have "shut out the lovely sunshine." She only half-heartedly believes that the shoals exist at all; her real conviction is that I am fussing over nothing. I shall have to convince her one of these days by putting her on to one of them; I have not hitherto done so of set purpose, and when sailing a month ago, I went aground in mid-channel, well up the Colne at L.W.S., for the excellent reason that there was no water anywhere to float us, her head appeared indignantly from the cabin (for the first time since Clacton) as the keel touched. She said that she had never known me do such a thing before. Her tone asked me what I meant by it.

But we must not forget that I was now under orders to return to the mooring. I went on deck, and tied up two reefs. I likewise bent the spitfire jib. Happily, the rain had abated, but the wind was whipping down the foam-streaked water in gusts that could be seen; they slit and tattered the surface of the waves. It was a joyless sail, but we lay snugly enough under the weather-shore when we reached the mooring, and the cabin was a warm and cosy spot for reading, for the writing of letters, and for the punctual service of *recherché* little meals. My lady was again herself, daintily clad, and well content.

II

Next morning, when I awoke, the sunlight was pouring through the skylight and portholes, and the little square of sky, visible through the skylight, was summer's own blue. What a change! The tide was rising smoothly; the water was slipping past us towards Maldon with a quiet air as if it had never misbehaved. It had clearly forgotten all about that turbulent grey welter of yesterday.

My shipmate came up from the cabin and looked about her with high approval. "Mersea to-day," she said. "I shall like to see Mersea again."

The wind came up with the tide from the south-east. The weather-shore had, of course, decamped again, but this fact did not disturb us, as the wind was not strong, and we were, moreover, outward bound. The reefs were shaken out, and we set sail.

I was 'forrard,' and my wife stood in the cockpit, bright in the sunshine, with the shadows of the rigging streaked across the sunlit white of her dress. She was handling the tiller with her accustomed efficiency.

"Slack off the fores'l sheet," I sang out.

The soliloquy in the cockpit, though spoken in an undertone, was loud enough to reach my ears:

"That's something *I've* got to do, but which string it is…"

We usually manage to contrive a species of 'reading without tears;' meaning is conveyed by signs and descriptions when the more technical language fails to convince her. It is another matter for compromise.

She, woman-like, imports into the little world of hemp and tar a certain delicacy of touch and a subtlety of perception which are all her own; her intuitions may have often the touch of genius; but at nautical phraseology she draws the line. I even suspect that she takes a wicked delight in some of her more egregious perversions. For a long time she had insisted upon calling jibs 'reefs.' My suggestion that their usual name is 'jib' was dismissed because "if they are not called reefs, they might just as well be, for one name is as good as another"—an argument to which, after all, there is no real answer.

So off we went at turn of the tide in the brisk little south-easterly breeze which had now sprung up, and we beat to and fro in the sunshine, with the ebb tide carrying us sideways on our voyage all the time. It was now afternoon; and although sailing is 'rather a waste of time,' and therefore superfluous, the kettle on the humming stove for tea is indispensable. The only real waste of time was the attempt to spread a tablecloth on the cabin top, because it merely blew off the moment it was put down; but tea was a great success, more especially as we were now past Osea, and were able, or nearly able, to lay our course close-hauled. And the sun shone down on the ruffled blue water, and the white foam bubbled past. It seemed an afternoon for indolent enjoyment, to stretch one's self out in the sunshine and to do nothing. I was therefore quite bewildered when I found that I was to be relieved of the tiller, and that my shipmate had elected of her free choice to steer the vessel. But in a moment I understood. I was told off to wash up the tea-things.

Before we reached the Nass Beacon, the 'quiet evenfall' had begun to steal upon us; and the wind was almost gone. But I was haunted with guilty doubt, for I know well that a berth in Mersea Quarters is no place for a south-easterly wind. The weather-shore is, moreover, no complete shelter, for the east wind brings up a swell from the sea, and the swell finds its way round the protective bank all the time. For the moment we were snug; the tidal weather-shore is an excellent one, and there was no swell to-night. With the banks uncovered, we should be sheltered this evening, but what of the morrow? Well, it is useless to meet trouble half-way; 'sufficient unto the day is the evil thereof,' and the anchor splashed into the water close up to the banks on the eastward shore. Sunset light now pervaded the whole scene. As the late dusk deepened into nightfall, the wind died altogether, and the reflections of rigging and riding lights of the few ships about us were traced in undulating patterns. Later, they became perfect images. The reflections were as silent and steady of outline as the quiet ships above them.

While I was busy furling the sails I heard sounds of stirring business below. The cabin lamp was alight and was shining brightly through the skylight. That was encouraging, for if the domestic authority once gets to work on the dinner, the dinner will always be good. The one drawback is that fresh water must be used for almost every process in refined cookery, a fact which in turn necessitates that breakers shall be carried ashore and refilled. At some places they charge one penny per 'breakerful,' not perhaps a ruinous charge in itself, but then there is sometimes twopence or threepence to be paid in addition, in order to induce the man with the key to come out of the public house and turn the water on. Fresh milk is another minor tribulation; it is not only required for culinary purposes, but (worse still) is essential to every cup of tea consumed. A cup of tea which had been defiled with preserved milk would be pronounced 'undrinkable.' I recall the wry face when the experiment has been forced upon us by unruly wind or inconsiderate tide.

Up came the bobstay and I went below. I was greeted effusively:

"Come along. Two small plates, four large ones, coffee-jugs, Oxo cubes, fish knives, forks and spoons, cups and saucers…"

That is only a beginning; but it is worth the turmoil, and when the meal is served and she asks triumphantly, "Now *isn't* that good?" I have no hesitation in my reply.

So our comfortable meal progressed, without even a thought about the washing up, because the dirty crockery will be stacked in the large tin basin and left for a general wash-up by daylight to-morrow. Finally, we turned out for a last look round. There was a great stillness. The land had disappeared completely, and the neighbouring riding lights were only faintly visible. We could not sit down anywhere, for the cabin top was thickly dabbled with moisture. A curtain of mist was enfolding us, and the moisture was dripping from the rigging. We were isolated in the little ring of the yellow gleam made by our riding light upon the mist about us. We were alone in the night.

Morning came ashen grey, with 'fold upon fold of hueless cloud,' but the surface mist had cleared, and a steady north-east wind was blowing. I chuckled. The weather had played the game for once. 'Good hunting,' as Mowgli said in the jungle. I enlarged upon the subject while I was cooking the bacon and eggs, until I nearly upset the pan. I was then told, in true connubial fashion, to "talk less and get on with the cooking."

The ebb was running briskly seaward, and we decided that we would go seaward likewise. When breakfast had been cleared, we set sail.

"I'm not such a fool as you make out," she said with her chin in the air, as I was hoisting the jib. "It's only to save myself the trouble of thinking of the right names. I know the right names. But why you should call the rope that you pull the sail up by a 'sheet,' I *don't* know."

"I generally call it a halliard."

She dropped the dignified air at once, and laughed. She is always off the mark before the flag goes down if ever there is a chance of a laugh at *me*, and if the case is reversed and the laugh is turned against herself she is equally ready. Her laugh is a laugh that makes the fortune of a very modest joke if she has once lent it her patronage; and so we went seaward in high humour.

After all, nautical language is by no means the only subject upon which my wife and I fail to see eye to eye. On the contrary, we have agreed to differ on almost every subject under the sun. We simply "agree to differ," and thus we remain, in Coventry Patmore's happy phrase: 'At inmost heart well pleased with one another.'

The horizons were hazy in spite of the breeze, and I laid a compass course for the Bench Head Buoy. To this day my shipmate inclines to think the Bench Head shoal a creature of my imagination, and that my refusal to lay a straight course for Colne Point is a bit of my nonsense.

"You don't really know as much about it as you try to make out," she says. "The fishing boats go straight."

"At high water they do, and so should we. It's low water now, or getting on that way." She did not combat it, but only yawned.

"I'm going below, there's no fun in this," she said, "and I don't like that dizzle on the water."

The 'dizzle' was a curious effect from 'cloud-clogged sunlight,' which made the water look ghostly in patches, and gave a queer sense of unreality to the whole seascape. The sun was trying to master the mist, but had not yet succeeded.

"I shall be quite happy; I shall read; you go on, you're enjoying it."

I was. There was a clean, steady breeze. The yacht was holding a comfortable course close-hauled, and the water was singing and bubbling past. The Bench Head Buoy jumped out of the haze right over the bowsprit, then the Bar, and I sailed on for Clacton. The wind was veering easterly, and the sea was now increasing. The haze had gone, and the sea was choppy.

I looked into the cabin to see if my shipmate were equally happy. She had forsaken the book, and was looking thoughtful.

"Not feeling very well?" I hazarded.

She looked at me pensively, and perhaps a trifle wanly, for a moment.

"We'll go ashore at West Mersea this afternoon," she affirmed with quiet decision.

The yacht changed course at once. Malaise was possible.

With the breeze freer and the tide rising, we sailed rapidly back.

"What did you say?" I leaned in toward the cabin expectantly.

"Why didn't you scald out the milk bottle this morning?"

The voice was one of obvious condemnation, but it was welcome. Clearly she was feeling quite herself again.

"Now are you sure it's Mersea you want to go to? The wind will be south-east as likely as not, and we shan't get any shelter. What about the weather-shore?"

"We won't come back on board till the tide goes down. Yes, Mersea. We'll have tea at the new tea-shop."

It was her own choice. And I know that, important though weather-shores may be, there is something more important in the feminine mind, and that is afternoon tea. When a plan of campaign for any afternoon is suggested, her first question is likely to be, "What about tea?" We have a tea-basket, with kettle and spirit-stove complete, for shore-going purposes when the shops fail us. I have carried it dozens of times in the aggregate. And seventy times seven I have scouted about to find a weather-shore for that stove. I may find a bank or wall directly between the stove and the wind, but derisive new draughts come swooping down for my special confusion, and blow the flame about anywhere and everywhere except upon the kettle—where it is wanted. And all the time I am asked, "Isn't that kettle boiling yet?" I am exasperated, because "If it were, I should say so without being asked; and when you know it isn't, what's the good of asking questions?" and so forth. Madam, prim in the background, will smile a smile of experience, and will say nothing. But when the kettle has fairly boiled, she will ask me, with a wicked twinkle, whether I am "feeling better."

Very well. I was absolved from responsibility for our anchorage; I was under contract for no weather-shore to-day. Back to Mersea Quarters we went. We donned our shore-going kit, and sailed the dinghy up to the causeway, where we left it in the charge of a small urchin. He would probably practise sailing in it all the afternoon, and would then get threepence from me afterwards for his trouble.

We were back on board at half-ebb; the banks had uncovered and we suffered no inconvenience.

Next morning we made ready for sea again. The sun was breaking through mist, and there was every prospect of a fine day. "Pin Mill?" I said.

"No," she replied, and left it at that. (The word was finality itself, and I did not pursue that proposal. The last time we went coastwise—to Aldeburgh it was, the railway was preferred for the return journey.)

"Where then?"

"Brightlingsea."

I set to work and made all ready. My fingers were busy on bobstay tackle to jib traveller outhaul and thence to tiers and halliards. All the time I felt that her eye had been following me; I know her far too well to imagine that she was admiring my dexterity, and at last she spoke:

"*Now* what's gone wrong? I know something has gone wrong because you're biting your nails." She is nothing if not unexpected, but that instinct of hers had

Back to Mersea Quarters we went

not led her far astray. The real fact was that a couple of smacks had anchored close up to us since we dropped our own hook; the channel was narrow, and they would certainly impede our freedom of action in getting away. I was very much aware of them, but was quite unconscious of having been 'biting my nails.'

So away we went and without trouble. The stem-post clove the blue water again, and the white foam went bubbling and singing away once more on both sides, while the dinghy following made her own bow-wave of sunlit white.

In idle contentment, we turned along the edge of the Mersea Flats, and reached up between the Cocum Hills and the Bench Head. After calling at Brightlingsea in the dinghy, we sailed higher up the Colne to anchor. In that kindly river, the weather-shore can always be found, in the Colne or Pyefleet Channel, blow the wind whence it will.

So our days passed. For two or three days the breeze had held easterly, which would give us a fair wind up the Blackwater. If we lingered we might have to beat, and perhaps in rough weather.

On a glorious morning therefore, with only a faint breeze from the N.E., the anchor was broken out, and we left the Colne on the tail of the ebb, and took the young flood up the Blackwater. So light was the wind that—until the tide turned in our favour—we hardly made progress at all. In clothing of the lightest, we enjoyed the sunshine on the blue sea; the Mersea smacks, picturesquely grouped together, were reflected perfectly in the quiet water—with sails of varied colour, reds and ochrous browns and warm greys. They were a picture. Gliding like a ghost, we were drawn by the still tide and light air past them. There was no sense of movement; on the contrary, we might have been anchored ourselves, and all these coloured objects have been moving smoothly and ceaselessly past. One began to feel drowsy.

The day had much in common with its immediate predecessors. It was of a fine weather type. The wind, north-easterly and light in the morning, had each day veered to south-eastward in the afternoon with the regularity of clockwork. It had blown freshly and even stiffly at top of the tide, dying away again completely at sunset or very shortly afterwards. To-day seemed likely to remain true to type.

Accordingly I set my wits to work upon my familiar problem. I selected the mouth of Lawling Creek as our anchorage, where the land would be close to us, and directly to the south-eastward. This would be so ideal a weather-shore that improvement would be impossible. It was pre-eminent. It was perfect.

The yacht rippled along merrily with the rising draught of wind in her sunlit mainsail; then the sheet was hauled in and she reached gracefully up the creek; finally she was shot up into the wind and the anchor was dropped.

This was good. I furled the sails contentedly, and sat down in the sunshine. It was a charming spot, with the farmhouse on the shore quite close at hand, and the blue creek running up landward beyond us into the sunlit fields.

An hour or two passed. I was quite confident of the issue, but I wished I had noted the *time* at which the wind had veered on previous days. I looked at my watch. The wind was certainly rising, but it was not south-easterly yet.

The mud-flats had covered, and we could get ashore in the dinghy. This was part of the programme. A walk of a mile or two would take us to a village, and we wanted to buy a few things. So off we went. No doubt the wind would have done its duty before we returned.

We returned in due course towards evening, having discharged our obligations. My wife said nothing as she got into the dinghy, but she just looked at me. There was no disguising the fact that the yacht was behaving in a remarkable fashion; when we left her she was staid and quiet, she was now rolling and tumbling about. She had, in fact, that clumsy appearance of a yacht lying with stern to weather. She was sheering about and waves were breaking against her counter.

It was vile perfidy on the part of the weather. The wind was blowing hard from the north-east, right up the creek against the ebb tide. The weather-shore had gone. We went on board in silence.

I fastened the dinghy's painter on the cleat, and looked down into the cabin. My shipmate was sitting down there, and not looking happy. It was a wretched moment. My weather-lore was supposed to be reliable; it was now an exploded myth.

I offered to shift, but she would not hear of it.

"It's getting late, and it's getting dark," she said wearily. "I shall turn in. Don't try to move. And the wind will drop; it has every night."

Yes, surely the wind would drop. The sky was clear of cloud, and there was no sign of a break in the fine weather, except for this driving, howling, relentless wind. I was glad not to move, for the tidal banks were just awash and the light failing. It would have been difficult to beat out without getting picked up.

The wind did *not* drop; it blew steadily and hard all night. My diary records "fine night all night, waning moon." That means that I was out half-a-dozen times in the night to see if we were dragging; for if I had not been on the *qui vive* I should never have seen that waning moon at all. The conditions were ideal for dragging, but happily that 'crown of sorrow' was not added to our tribulations. The whole thing is an evil memory. There had not been one flicker of humour to relieve the glumness of our period of endurance.

Morning was clear and brilliantly sunny, and the tide was ebbing fast. The wind was still right up the creek, and we had thumped and bumped unmercifully all night. There was no thought of breakfast. We got the sails on her, and thrashed to and fro, to and fro, on the preposterously short boards which the narrowness of the channel enforced, and then turned gladly westward, until the protective line of Osea Island lay comfortably sprawled out between us and that detestable wind. Never was I more glad to find a weather-shore. Moreover, it was daylight now, and even if the wind *did* begin boxing the compass for our confusion, we could shift and shift again; we would continue dancing round the mulberry bush all day to dodge it if necessary. A weather-shore we would have—a weather-shore based on the realities of the moment, and not upon suppositions of the future.

"Well, you're a nice one."

The voice struck a merry note; it was a relief after the rather strained utterances of the past twelve hours.

I hardly needed to look at her pleased and mischievous face to know that I was now likely to hear certain truths. My complicated explanations were soon abandoned, and I took refuge behind the frying pan and cooking fork. After all, one must have breakfast!

Fate had ordained that we were to be confined to the upper Blackwater for the two or three days that remained. Wind north-easterly can knock up an amazing sea on the ebb below Osea. We beat down this very morning to sample it, with two reefs down. But every wave came right over the stem-post, and everything on deck was running water. It seemed wonderful that so much wind should come out of a cloudless sky. My shipmate threatened a complete bout of *mal-de-mer* if we kept on; I knew it was only an idle threat, but I put the tiller up, and we made love to the weather-shore again.

I knew it was only an idle threat, and she has since frankly admitted that her chief anxiety was a fear that I might fall overboard in the rough water. Very touching and proper—if she had left it at that. But she did not.

"I was so afraid that you might fall overboard, and then I shouldn't have known in the least what to do. I *couldn't* have got the yacht back alone."

It is unconsciously a repetition of that story told by Frank Cowper, who did actually go overboard when he had a couple of visitors on his yacht. It recalls their white-faced comment when he scrambled back, thanks to the sheets which he had never let go. "Oh, Cowper, what *should* we have done?"

We went up to Maldon and down again, called at Heybridge Basin and returned, and frittered away our time in perfect happiness. Then we picked up the mooring buoy, and I—rather sadly—put the cover on the mainsail again.

"Well, that's that. I hope you've enjoyed it?"

Her reply, totally unexpected, but apparently serious, sticks in my memory. "You have been very polite."

I am afraid that it throws a lurid sidelight upon my conduct ashore. But at all events we had been very happy, and our hunting of the weather-shore had been successful in the main, in spite of one or two disastrous failures. Her gracious presence, Beata Mea Domina, upon the old workaday yacht, is a consecration and a delight; but I dare not tell her so, for she would only ask me whether I was waiting to borrow half-a-crown. And so our ten days were ended.

*   *   *

In case I were meanly taking an advantage, having recorded my own version of our doings, while the chief figure in the drama had no opportunity of rejoinder, I produced the MS one autumn evening by the fireside and told my wife that I would read it aloud to her. She looked up from her book, and her glance was a glance of patience.

"Well, if I've got to listen," she said, "you must wait while I fetch my needle-work."

The phrase 'got to listen' did not sound auspicious, but she lived it down at once by her obvious interest and quick laughter.

"Think it's good?" I modestly inquired, expectant, author-like, of incense.

"*I* should say," she replied, with fine impartiality, "that it was absolute drivel."

She resembles the great Apostle of the Gentiles in one respect if in no other, for she 'uses great plainness of speech.' Perhaps I hope inwardly that, as a deliberate verdict, my wife's generalisation is a trifle too sweeping, but I will have the grace to leave the last word with her, to whom, after all, the 'last word' is an hereditary right.

The Way of Peace

I

"YOU'RE 'CUSTOMED TO SAILIN', SIR."

He was standing on the bank beside the little yacht and had watched me tying up a reef in the mainsail. I had just gone on board at Wroxham, and perhaps I was looking more adequate and businesslike than I felt.

"Yes," I replied, "but not to ditches."

He smiled confidentially. "Y'know a sight more about it than most on 'em. Them other two lots?" His tone touched a note of derision, as he continued with an appreciative chuckle. "Them other two lots? The ole toff, 'e doano much. An' the other gen'lman? Why, *look at 'im*." The tone was more eloquent than any words.

My manner of handling reef points had evidently betrayed me as an old hand. But I was a stranger here. It had occurred to me to try Broadland for a week or so. I was at this moment taking over a hired yacht, and the 'busy housewife' was at work in the cabin; she was storing a mixed freight from the basket brought down by the grocer's boy.

I had expected to be woefully irked for want of elbow room in these narrow rivers—hence my reference to 'ditches.' It was not meant by way of disparagement or (Heaven knows) of patronage; my feeling was not that I was too big for these waters, but that these waters would not be big enough for me. I had indeed expected to make a fool of myself. But now, after watching the 'ole toff who doano much,' I began to pluck up heart of grace. A stranger like myself need not be conspicuous, even if clumsy.

"Ready, sir?" The man gave the yacht a shove, I hauled in the sheet, and she was off.

A strong breeze was blowing; but we were so much mewed in here and blanketed by trees that she often lost it altogether. Nevertheless, the first touch of the tiller was enough to send anyone's anxieties packing. She was so sensitive and so instantly responsive that she seemed to look after herself.

"Thank goodness to be off." My shipmate smiled in her complete contentment, glad to be under way. The two of us were really like children with a new

Sunset

toy, and, as we turned to windward between the massed foliage, my first effort of helmsmanship was promptly concluded.

"Lem-me."

I was deposed. I held the mainsheet and sang out "lee-ho!" or "let her come!" about four or five times to the minute, or so it seemed, for we were turning dead to windward in that ridiculous little alleyway of water.

"Call this sailing?" my helmswoman chuckled. "*I* call it wriggling."

There was no long curve of the long-keeled boat; this little boat did her twist at once and had done with it. She would be quite happy to double back on her tracks in her own length.

And there was no need to think ahead. There was no anxiety as to saving one's tide nor as to finding a snug berth in sheltered water for the night, and any sudden drop of the barometer didn't matter. This comfort and security of the Broads was beginning to appeal to us.

The trees, growing close down to the water's edge on both sides, robbed us of that romping wind which drove the cloud masses helter-skelter across the blue. But the little draught that reached us was sufficient to send us rippling on; now it was a reach, now a twist and wriggle to windward, barely progressing, and then with a whish the wind would swoop through some opening, and lay the little packet over, as she raced through the water. Then again the rippling noise round her bows would die to silence all in a moment; and, upright in the water, she would be gliding soundlessly on, through the dark green reflections of the matted trees. "Isn't it time for tea?"

It certainly was. Tea was much overdue. We had reached the entrance to Salhouse Broad, and there we moored while the kettle boiled. I had filled the kettle from the stone jar, an article which was easily the crudest item in the boat inventory. After being accustomed to accessible tanks with a decent tap, this jar which had to be unlashed from the rudder stem and relashed after use was an abomination. And the small size of the jar showed that frequent fillings would be necessary. But we were always 'in touch with the shore,' and we could wash in water brought in from over the side.

In the meantime, while we lingered at tea, the big spaces of blue above had vanished. The rippled water had lost its life. Ruffled it was, but in this dull evening it looked almost muddy. The wind had increased body, and the sky was lowering. We pushed off, and decided that we were not bound far. We would just find a snug anchorage for the night; there was no encouragement to press on.

The wind was noisy in the trees; "the rooks were blown about the skies" and a cloudy evening was now closing down. So we squirmed and twisted forward; and this boisterous wind, running mostly to riotous waste above, caught us a sudden buffet now and again, and slapped us angrily along.

Change came in an instant when we had espied our berth for the night; we were stock still beside the bank, and there was a great calm. The shelter from trees to windward was complete. It was miraculous, a magical change. The rod anchors were made fast, the sails furled, and the cabin top raised. We were moored for the night.

The light from the cabin lamp shone more and more brightly through the portholes as I finished putting on the sail cover. Night was closing down, and the dark banks and water were becoming blurred. With a feeling of utter strangeness I stepped ashore from the deck of the yacht and reboarded her aft.

I went below. It looked a homely and cheerful little place, as a cabin always does on a dirty night; and it was a firm and stationary cabin too, unlike that of a yacht on the salt water in this weather. I stretched out my legs under the table and lounged contentedly as I listened to the blast; no snubbing of the cable on the bitt-heads, no sudden grinding on the bobstay, not even a whine and howling in the shrouds and a devil's tattoo in the rigging. It was absolute peace.

Supper was cleared, and I stepped out into the well to look round at the night. My breath caught and stopped and my heart almost missed a beat—we had dragged our anchor and were aground! It was an instantaneous effect, a ridiculous misgiving, but it certainly gave me a start. The clipped reeds close beside us looked in the faint light like a shoal just awash. I laughed outright. The contrast suggested by that momentary shock lent but a greater zest to our present serenity. It was 'the way of peace.'

Then I turned in and made myself useful. Washing up in the well is not a welcome task by night, but it is detestable if left for the morning. So I accepted the lesser evil and did the job. I then tossed the water overboard with a merry splash. *The bubbles stayed there*; they did not budge. One is accustomed to see the little grey patch of bubbles snatched away into the night by the swift tide, and lost at once in the dark water astern. But here, they just stayed there, and blinked and burst one by one without having moved a single inch from where they first 'bubbled.'

The night clouds rifted, and a half moon peered between them, but was lost again. Another silvered patch followed, and another quick gleam; and then the whole landscape was dim and dark.

So we turned in. Drowsy and well-content I drew up the blankets over me in my bunk, still listening to the anger of the wind. On the verge of sleep I could still hear it, and the ripple of the water. Then, on a sudden, I was stark awake with a guilty start—I had turned in without putting up the riding light! Again I smiled at the evidence of my upbringing, and turned over and went to sleep in earnest.

Morning came. We awoke to the sound of wind, but we also awoke to the golden colour of sunshine. The sky seen through the portholes was heavenly blue. I

We were in the Broads

was soon busy at my cooking in the open well, with one appreciative eye all the while upon the rippled water and the waving rushes close at hand. There certainly was 'security' about it all; here was the wind whistling and whooping over the tree-tops, and we were in a windless haven of refuge.

Beyond our sheltered mooring, the river took a right-angled turn beyond us, and the wind was coming straight down that reach that lay round the corner. Little foam-capped waves, quite spiteful little things, were breaking its surface, and making a regular storm in a teacup. The look of the water suggested two reefs, and I pulled them down. They were wanted.

So we pushed off. Without jib, and under this little pocket handkerchief of reefed mainsail only, we set forth for our first experience of turning dead to windward in really strong wind on one of these narrow streams. Neither board was the better board; the wind was dead ahead. But the little boat knew her business and ran to and fro in a manner fit to gladden anybody's heart. With careful handling she shot well into the eye of the wind as she went about; and quite amusing it seemed to be putting the helm down when her bows were virtually ashore and to come about with her stern actually brushing the rushes. *Whish* came the wind, and the tugging main-sheet bit into one's hand as she heeled, fetching across to the green bank opposite in a single instant; up she came, slatting as she spilled the wind and quivering in her very timbers as the little waves broke upon her thin-built bows, and then lying away on the other track and racing again to those tall green rushes. But all in a moment, the busy scene had vanished. We were basking in hot sunshine, we were becalmed in a windless atmosphere. We had reached Horning Staithe, and the buildings shut off the wind completely. We moored and looked about us.

After a brief interval, we were again away. Being bound eastward against the easterly wind, we expected to sail close-hauled, for as yet we were wholly lacking in Broadland instinct. In a few minutes, however, we were racing down upon Horning Ferry, full before the wind, and steering watchfully, on the delicate border of a gybe. In came the mainsheet and on she drove. It was all a joy. Opposite the dyke to Ranworth Broad we paused for lunch, and then we lingered—revelling in the feast of colour. The tall church tower was blue in the shadow, but the banks were living green and a path of sunlight was golden upon the water.

On again we sailed, and below Horning Church we broke cover from these wooded lands. Here was a spacious landscape with its distant church towers, its mills, its few white sails, and stretching away the line of horizon blue.

The wind was right down the Ant. A yacht was sailing down under headsail only, her white jib and yellow mast, strongly sunlit, were bright against the living blue of the sky. We foamed across her bows with ample margin, and sped onward past St. Benet's Abbey.

Here we moored. A great wherry lay beside us, with her sturdy and gaily-bedizened mast high above our own insignificant little yellow pole.

It is always a disappointment, after a good sunset, to awaken to a grey world in the morning. Under heavy cloud we made our way to Potter Heigham, and I ventured my first effort at lowering the mast. The task proved, of course, to be simplicity itself. We were soon moored beyond the railway bridge. I replaced the jaws of the gaff upon the mast, and, as I picked up the parrel-line to re-fasten it, I was mentally computing what length it ought to be given; but, as usual, there was no room for doubt. A knot had been tied at the proper place. The instance is a small one, but things are really so much simplified and standardised on the Broads that it is almost impossible to make mistakes.

A paid hand from another yacht had sauntered up; he lingered and we chatted.

"Lot of wind yesterday and the day before," I said as I cleated the forestay. "Where were you?"

"I didn't get under way at all. No fear. Not me. It'd blow the mast out of my boat." "Going through to Hickling now?"

"No. Can't get there. See that chimney up there? I shan't go no further. It ain't fit for any boat to go. The mud."

On hearing that I was bound for Horsey Mere, he advised me to bring up at the self-same chimney, and go on (if go on I must) in the dinghy.

"It's all mud, you're bound to stick. Take my advice."

He sauntered off and got under way. He brought up at his chimney; and there I watched him once and again. He stretched two awnings over well and bows respectively, and turned his company loose in the dinghy while he sat and kept watch and ward over the yacht. Possibly he had suggested the propriety of their visiting Heigham Sounds, Hickling Broad, Horsey Mere, and Martham Broad while he sat and smoked and kept the yacht from running away.

This Broadland sailing did not call out one's stern virtues. The beginner, unless he is really rash and silly, can safely go careering about to his heart's content: he can charge the rushes, and he can mix himself in his sheets and halliards without any injury, save his pride. Whenever he has had enough sailing, he can just stop. The banks are all around him. If any of his gear carries away, he can tie up to the bank and take stock of his situation in peace and safety.

Our mast was by this time re-stepped, and we were ready to push forward again into the unknown.

II

The sun broke through in the afternoon. We had to turn to windward up Heigham Sound in a narrow channel between towering grasses that cover most of the Broad. The long landscape was gone; a little world of yellow jungle and blue water had swallowed us.

A wherry was just ahead, reefed down

This solitude was broken for a moment as we emerged and opened the entrance to Hickling Broad. A rush-laden boat was being rapidly poled along by a shaggy-looking man who might have been a Saxon serf.

"No good holding further on this board," I said, "let her come."

"Come? She won't 'come,' as you call it. She's stuck, rudder and all. There you are, *stuck*, just like the man said you would be." We both laughed.

The bottom was covered with a dense growth of woolly-looking brownish weed, through which the keel was generally able to make its way, though much retarded. The actual channel into Old Meadow Dyke is very narrow, but the quant pole can be quite a useful weapon, and we now entered the narrow waterway.

The short-lived sunshine had gone. Having emerged from the reed-grown mere, we had opened up the fenland levels again. The wind had fallen lighter, and we stole silently through the twilight over a still surface. The whole mere seemed to be reed-bordered and desolate of life, edged round with fringes of swamp. One or two lonely birds winged across the grey sky, uttering a disconsolate call.

We were in doubt whether or not we would return to Old Meadow Dyke; but, as we did so, we heard the splash of oars. A row boat was crossing the mere and we lay hove to awaiting it.

"Is there any place to moor hereabout?"

"Ay, there's the staithe down there, and there's a high road nigh agenst it. You follow us. We're on our way there now."

The idea of a high road was welcome. We followed. An unexpected opening between the long fringes of reed brought us to a narrow fleet and a solid bank; and in a few minutes after mooring, the lamp was alight in the cabin and a savoury meal was merrily cooking on the stove.

When morning came, I looked out from the sleepy cabin. The well was littered with little melting hailstones, and a cloud, dark and ragged, was over half the sky, but was closing down toward the horizon. To windward was a break of heavenly blue, and a range of cloud like Alpine summits. It was a sudden hail squall which had awakened me, and in a few moments the sun was shining.

For once we were in no hurry to get the cover off the mainsail; we thought we would walk down to the sea. We shut down the cabin, and made our way on foot toward the heaped sandhills that mark the shore-line.

Fresh from our Broadland rivers we crossed the sandhills and reached the deserted shore and the edge of the heavily breaking surf. Here, strewn along the beach was wreckage of broken wood and there were *onions*. Far away a solitary figure moved, and as it drew nearer we saw that it was a wild-looking creature with a sack, collecting relics of this wasted cargo. This was a real contrast to our winding streams and reedy pools. The waves broke, the seagulls hovered and curved, and the wind sang.

Our little burgee, fluttering among the trees, was sighted as we walked back along the road, and we were soon on board. The day was now a day of blue sky and driven white cloud; and we were away in the afternoon, reefed as usual, and were soon racing across the open mere. Horsey Mere in sunlight, with its waters broken into blue wavelets, and fringed by yellow reed, was delightful.

The little yacht flew through the narrow dyke, seemingly able to take any corner and curve at any pace she pleased. Past Heigham Sounds she scudded, and back into the Thurne, heading now for Martham Broad. Was there any way through? Where was it? She seemed to be racing to a flat dead end; the river seemed to have come to a complete stop unless something opened out. We glanced eagerly to left and right, and there was nothing. But, as I put the helm down and sent her slatting into the wind, the answer dawned upon us. A floating bridge had been set across the river for a farm-cart to pass over, and we had only to wait a few minutes. We soon went rippling onward again. We moored in the river, close to an old windmill, and there we spent the evening in lazy content.

But the morning that followed had little golden quality about it. Wind was of gale force and a tearing rain was pitting the water and deluging the banks. I merely saw to it that the well-awning was doing its duty and keeping out the rain, and we stayed inside out of the wet.

We went ashore in the afternoon, and got thoroughly wet, and were glad to be back in the cabin, well-housed, warmly clad, and snug at a well-laid table under the bright little cabin lamp.

Next morning there was no rain, but there was a wind which hurtled us at speed, reefed down though we were. So we flew off to Acle. A wherry was just ahead of us as we entered the Bure, reefed down so much and heeling to the wind to such an extent that she began to look unwherry-like. We could sail her pace, but, as for keeping to weather, we were nowhere in the same class. Right up against the reeds of the weather side, actually brushing against them, and following into every indentation of the bank, she slid along in a manner that was marvellous.

At Acle Bridge we turned back, bound for the Ant. The bridge was passed, and we wound our way past willows and rushy borders and water-side windmills, and finally passed the wharf at Irstead Street. A wherry was loading there, and the men passed the time of day with us cheerily. Night was falling by the time that we moored half a mile or so above Ludham Bridge. Black in the twilight, the great sail of a wherry loomed up. Round the corner she swung, incredibly close to the wind, with the great block at the clew of her mainsail sheeted hard down right amidships. Out came the quant pole, and the man put his shoulder and all his weight upon it, as he followed it down the deck, his feet tap-tap-tapping as he ran—for the wherry was carrying way and no mistake. His fellow steered in the scanty cockpit, and there were lights from the little windows of the cabin.

"You're perfect marvels," I said as the helmsman passed close beside me.

"How so?" said he, pleased.

"The way you keep to weather."

"Ah, it's the old wherry," he said, "*she* knows. She lives up at Irstead. She knows her way up to Irstead Street. She knows her way home."

So, as the days followed, we wandered on to South Walsham Broad, Horning Staithe and Salhouse; and the river above Wroxham had a charm of its own. It was a delightful time, and quite a revelation.

* * *

Salt-water men, as a rule, are inclined to eye the Broads askance, and its fresh-water sailing; they have 'no use for it.' And, of course, it is unadventurous when compared with salt-water cruising, for it is so very sheltered. But there is plenty of busy and active sailing, and delightful landscape. It has a very real joy of its own.

In a Temperance Hotel (long ago in my young days) I noticed that—among the usual praises in the Visitors' Book—one entry was extremely warm. It ended, however, with the words: "But now I am off for a mild and bitter." Perhaps that is like the feeling of the salt-water sailor, on leaving the Broads. He doesn't like the softer life.

Back to the Sea

I MET MY OLD SHIPMATE AGAIN on the next week-end. He was somewhat sarcastic about the Broads, the more because he had never sailed there; but we were both merry about everything. Here was the salt water.

We set sail. The wind was north-east, and the passage to Mersea Quarters was slow, despite the strong ebb tide. We brought up inside the Nass in the twilight, we hung the riding light on the forestay, and turned in for supper. We were as snug as anyone could wish, but we noticed that the glass had been falling rapidly. We made sure that everything was taut and tidy, and we turned in and slept.

In the night the tide came up, and the yacht pitched and rolled, and the wind whistled. Only half-awake, I heard and felt it all; then the alarm clock did its work. We turned out in the gloomy twilight of the morning, and the whole picture was dull and desolate. It seemed that we were in for a rough day. We wanted the ebb tide to carry us to Harwich, so we pulled down two reefs in the mainsail, and we rummaged in the sail locker for the spitfire jib.

After a breakfast of sorts, we got our anchor and set sail. In an hour we were out of the estuary and in the open sea; above us there was a low scudding mass of dark cloud; the wind was bitter cold, and the sea was a foamy lather of steep and vicious waves. None the less, the morning was bracing and full of vigour—a splendid sail. We had passed the pier of Clacton, and were racing northward.

Then came a crack and a snap like a pistol shot. What was it? We soon saw: there was the dinghy broken loose; bobbing and lurching away, she looked very puny and helpless—now thrown up on the crests of the waves, and now hidden in the trough. In a moment the helm was put down, and the yacht close-hauled. It was easy enough to bring the yacht alongside the little cockleshell of a boat, but to get hold of her was a very different matter. When the yacht was on the top of the wave, the dinghy was in the trough, some ten feet below; and when the yacht was in the trough, the dinghy seemed most often to be up on the crest. It took us a rare long time to get hold of her, and it would have been mighty easy to tumble into the ditch during our busy efforts. To grab hold of the dinghy would have been sure to find one's own self pulled overboard, *promptissimo*. We finally managed the job by getting the kedge into her, and the task of getting her in tow was even then a difficult matter. But at last the truant was secured with two tough painters, and we sighed a sigh of relief. We were ashamed of ourselves for our carelessness; it was unforgivable on a day like this, and I don't think that we ever again were guilty of that omission.

Past Walton and the Naze we sailed onward. On the foam-capped waves the yacht rose, and slid down into the trough; this was quite regular, and was more and more quiet as we passed Harwich. We had a call to make at Ipswich; and up the Orwell and past Pin Mill, we sailed swiftly. We reached Ipswich before mid-day; and then the rain came on. We tied up to a post, waiting for the turn of the tide. In the late afternoon we dropped down the Orwell again, and anchored off Shotley. The sun was breaking through the clouds in the late evening, and the wind had fallen to a light breeze. All was peaceful and perfect, and we sat on the cabin-top, and enjoyed it to the utmost. At last I hung the riding light on the forestay. We turned in early, because we intended to sail again in the morning twilight, and to resume our little cruise northward along the coast. The old game, delightful as ever.

At last I hung the riding light on the forestay; we turned in